Promoting Student Success Through Group Interventions

∞ ALL HAWORTH BOOKS & JOURNALS
ARE PRINTED ON CERTIFIED
ACID-FREE PAPER

Promoting Student Success Through Group Interventions

Joseph E. Zins
Maurice J. Elias
Editors

The Haworth Press, Inc.
New York • London • Norwood (Australia)

Promoting Student Success Through Group Interventions has also been published as *Special Services in the Schools*, Volume 8, Number 1, 1993.

Paperback edition published in 1995.

The Haworth Press, Inc., 10 Alice Street, Binghamton, NY 13904-1580, USA

Library of Congress Cataloging-in-Publication Data

Promoting student success through group interventions / Joseph E. Zins, Maurice J. Elias, editors.
p. cm.
Includes bibliographical references (p.).
ISBN 1-56024-507-7
1. Educational counseling. 2. Group counseling. 3. Student assistance programs. 4.Students–Services for. I. Zins, Joseph E. II. Elias, Maurice J.
LB 1027.5 P676 1993
371'.4'6–dc20 93-42447
CIP

INDEXING & ABSTRACTING

Contributions to this publication are selectively indexed or abstracted in print, electronic, online, or CD-ROM version(s) of the reference tools and information services listed below. This list is current as of the copyright date of this publication. See the end of this section for additional notes.

- ***Child Development Abstracts & Bibliography***, University of Kansas, 2 Bailey Hall, Lawrence, KS 66045
- ***Contents Pages in Education***, Carfax Information Systems, P.O. Box 25, Abingdon, Oxfordshire OX14 3UE, United Kingdom
- ***Education Digest***, Prakken Publications, Inc., 416 Longshore Drive/P.O. Box 8623, Ann Arbor, MI 48107
- ***Educational Administration Abstracts***, Sage Publications, Inc., 2455 Teller Road, Newbury Park, CA 91320
- ***ERIC Clearinghouse on Rural Education & Small Schools***, Appalachia Educational Laboratory, 1031 Quarrier Street, P.O. Box 1348, Charleston, WV 25325
- ***Exceptional Child Education Resources (ECER) (online through DIALOG and hard copy)***, The Council for Exceptional Children, 1920 Association Drive, Reston, VA 22091
- ***International Bulletin of Bibliography on Education***, Proyecto B.I.B.E./Apartado 52, San Lorenzo del Escorial, Madrid, Spain

(continued)

- ***Inventory of Marriage and Family Literature (online and hard copy)***, National Council on Family Relations, 3989 Central Avenue NE, Suite 550, Minneapolis, MN 55421

- ***Mental Health Abstracts (online through DIALOG)***, IFI/Plenum Data Company, 3202 Kirkwood Highway, Wilmington, DE 19808

- ***National Clearinghouse for Bilingual Education***, George Washington University, 1118 22nd Street NW, Washington, DC 20037

- ***OT BibSys***, American Occupational Therapy Foundation, P.O. Box 1725, Rockville, MD 20849-1725

- ***Psychological Abstracts (PsycINFO)***, American Psychological Association, P.O. Box 91600, Washington, DC 20090-1600

- ***Social Work Research & Abstracts***, National Association of Social Workers, 750 First Street NW, 8th Floor, Washington, DC 20002

- ***Sociology of Education Abstracts***, Carfax Publishing Company, P.O. Box 25, Abingdon, Oxfordshire OX14 3UE, United Kingdom

- ***Special Educational Needs Abstracts***, Carfax Information Systems, P.O. Box 25, Abingdon, Oxfordshire OX14 3UE, United Kingdom

- ***Urban Affairs Abstracts***, National League of Cities, 1301 Pennsylvania Avenue NW, Washington, DC 20004

(continued)

SPECIAL BIBLIOGRAPHIC NOTES

related to indexing, abstracting, and library access services

- ❑ indexing/abstracting services in this list will also cover material in the "separate" that is co-published simultaneously with Haworth's special thematic journal issue or DocuSerial. Indexing/abstracting usually covers material at the article/chapter level.
- ❑ monographic co-editions are intended for either non-subscribers or libraries which intend to purchase a second copy for their circulating collections.
- ❑ monographic co-editions are reported to all jobbers/wholesalers/approval plans. The source journal is listed as the "series" to assist the prevention of duplicate purchasing in the same manner utilized for books-in-series.
- ❑ to facilitate user/access services all indexing/abstracting services are encouraged to utilize the co-indexing entry note indicated at the bottom of the first page of each article/chapter/contribution.
- ❑ this is intended to assist a library user of any reference tool (whether print, electronic, online, or CD-ROM) to locate the monographic version if the library has purchased this version but not a subscription to the source journal.
- ❑ individual articles/chapters in any Haworth publication are also available through the Haworth Document Delivery Services (HDDS).

ABOUT THE EDITORS

Joseph E. Zins, EdD, is Professor in the College of Education at the University of Cincinnati. Also a psychologist, he has published extensively in the areas of prevention and the delivery of psychological services in educational settings.

Maurice J. Elias, PhD, is a psychologist and Associate Professor in the Department of Psychology at Rutgers University. He has published widely in the area of prevention and is the co-author of several curricula for social problem solving.

Zins and Elias are both fellows of the American Psychological Association and members of the Consortium on the School-Based Promotion of Social Competence.

Promoting Student Success Through Group Interventions

CONTENTS

Promoting Student Competence Through School-Based Group Interventions: An Introduction

Joseph E. Zins
University of Cincinnati

Maurice J. Elias
Rutgers University

SUMMARY. There is a growing need for school-based interventions which address students' social, affective, and life skills. Group interventions provide an efficient complement to more prevalent individual and consultative approaches. Contributors to this volume share specific intervention techniques applied to diverse student populations and problem areas, as well as the conceptual underpinnings of their approaches. Particular consideration is given to multicultural influences on group interventions and ways to stabilize intervention procedures to ensure maximal treatment integrity and responsiveness to changes in students and circumstances. In this article, we provide an overview of how

---

Address correspondence to: Dr. Joseph E. Zins, Department of Early Childhood and Special Education, 339 Teachers College, University of Cincinnati, Cincinnati, OH 45221-0002.

[Haworth co-indexing entry note]: "Promoting Student Competence Through School-Based Group Interventions: An Introduction." Zins, Joseph E., and Maurice J. Elias. Co-published simultaneously in *Special Services in the Schools* (The Haworth Press, Inc.) Vol. 8, No. 1, 1993, pp. 1-7; and: *Promoting Student Success Through Group Interventions* (ed: Joseph E. Zins, and Maurice J. Elias) The Haworth Press, Inc., 1993, pp. 1-7. Multiple copies of this article/chapter may be purchased from The Haworth Document Delivery Center [1-800-3-HAWORTH; 9:00 a.m. - 5:00 p.m. (EST)].

this volume on school-based group interventions designed to promote students' social and academic success is organized to assist service providers in effectively utilizing this critical and needed modality.

GROUP INTERVENTIONS: AN INTRODUCTION

The purpose of this volume is to provide clear, concise, and practical descriptions of group interventions designed to promote student success in school and in life. Abundant opportunities and requirements to participate in groups exist for most school-aged children. These include clubs, teams, and committees, as well as regular and special education classes (Claiborn, Kerr, & Strong, 1990). Unfortunately, however, ineffective participation in these activities can result in negative outcomes for students.

Traditionally, special services professionals have focused their efforts on interventions and procedures such as counseling and more recently consultation, directed toward assisting individual students, and this mode of operation continues to dominate their practices. Furthermore, the professional literature tends to be replete with descriptions of individually-focused intervention approaches; reviews of group interventions are found far less frequently. Moreover, discussions with colleagues confirm our observations that it is common for many graduate training programs for special services providers to place less emphasis on group-based approaches to assisting students in contrast to individual approaches. Finally, although we are not advocating that group interventions replace those that are individually-focused (i.e., there will always be a need for individual counseling and psychotherapy), we are convinced by the growing incidence of violence, poverty, stress-related disorders, and related problem behaviors among children and youth (Tuma, 1989) that there is a critical need to expand the numbers of children and youth who receive health and mental health promotion services in the schools. Group interventions are one means for special services staff to reach the increasing number of students who require assistance.

Further, there are a growing number of mandates to provide an array of services to prevent the onset of problems such as AIDS, drug and alcohol use or abuse, and smoking, as well as to promote healthy life styles and the kinds of skills needed for responsible participation in the key social roles of citizen, family member, and member of the work force (Elias, 1993; Elias & Tobias, 1990). Students receiving special services cannot be exempted or omitted from programs directed toward these goals (although too often, they are), and there can be little doubt that the expertise of special services providers will be tapped to assist schools' overall efforts in these areas. For these reasons, we believe that this volume is timely, and that it will be helpful to special services providers who desire to expand the range of their professional influence by targeting interventions to greater numbers of students.

A variety of carefully selected group-based interventions are described. Stewart Ehly provides an informative overview of considerations that underlie all group interventions, regardless of the type of student or background or orientation of the service provider. Specific interventions in the areas of children of divorce (Neil Kalter & Shelly Schreier), children who have been bereaved (Mary Ann Healy-Romanello), and children who have been labeled as having attention deficit-hyperactivity disorder (ADHD) or related disruptive behavior problems (Lauren Braswell) are our main problem-oriented foci. While by no means exhaustive, these topics were chosen because they are appropriate for school-based practitioners, they address child-related problems that special services professionals frequently confront, and they have a solid theoretical and/or empirical foundation supporting their utilization.

We also focus on two group intervention approaches to promoting positive adjustment (and thus valuable for a preventive focus): peer leadership training (Sharon Rose Powell) and group social skills interventions (Frank Gresham and Stephen Elliott). There is broad power and applicability of each of these approaches, both for children who already have a sound skill base but for whom preparation for future challenges is desired, and those who are in need of these interventions as ways to remediate learning and/or behavior problems. We should note, however, that although the interventions in this volume tend to be described with students as the primary targets of the interventions and the reader as the group leader, we do not mean to exclude the idea that teachers, other professionals, and, at times, parents can be trained to carry out these programs. Later in this article, we discuss this point, as well as how special services providers also can engage in group-based peer support activities to enhance their professional skills.

The articles are directed toward a variety of school practitioners including school psychologists, counselors, special educators, administrators, and related professionals who potentially may be involved at some level in the implementation of these procedures. To meet the needs of this audience, the articles are written by experts who have extensive experience in the application of these procedures with children and families in educational and related settings. Therefore, there is an emphasis upon describing practical procedures in sufficient detail to enable their adoption and replication.

Moreover, it has been our experience that many of the group (as well as other) interventions presented in the literature are inadequately described, and thus open to interpretation regarding how they might be implemented in local settings (Lippitt, Langseth, & Mossop, 1986). Although the dissemination of effective programs involves a complex array of issues well beyond the scope of this special issue (see Bauman, Stein, & Ireys, 1991), it will not occur without adequate descriptions of the intervention programs. Readers will find sufficient guidance from the contributors to allow them to select models and procedures with which they feel comfortable, and they also will find materials to enable them to carry through at least a sample of the interventions to see how they will work in the readers' particular context.

In general, the articles are organized to include an overview of the theoretical and instructional bases for the approach, including an outline of the purpose of the program, target population(s), age/grade levels, problems/risk factors addressed, and format(s) for which the use of the program is best suited. A brief description of how to determine an organization's readiness for the program is included in several articles. They also include a step-by-step outline of what is done in the program and an explanation of the instructional/therapeutic/counseling procedures used to effect behavioral change. Many detailed points of how to get started (i.e., running the first session or two, establishing rules, facilitating group cohesion, attendance issues, etc.) are given explicit attention.

Methods to assess learner outcomes or benefits to group members are also made explicit. Included are issues such as satisfaction, knowledge, attitudes, and skills or behavioral change. Reasons why readers should consider adoption of the approaches are provided in several articles. Although each program's rationale varies, reasons include the authors' outcome data, monitoring of practice, supporting research from others, theoretical literature, or some combination. It is recognized that some of the approaches have substantial empirical data demonstrating their effectiveness, while others offer much promise for success, even though they may not have been extensively validated through repeated empirical investigations at this point in their development. We believe that readers will be impressed with the efforts that have been taken to evaluate the programs, particularly because a number of them are conducted by practitioners whose evaluation efforts are not funded by outside agencies or directed by university-based researchers.

In this volume, groups can refer to a subset of children within a classroom, children from an entire classroom, or subsets of children from several classrooms or schools. As a rule, the interventions are not directed toward bringing about organizational change within entire schools or school districts, although that may be necessary as part of the process of implementing the program and to generalize outcomes. Indeed, Mary Jane Rotheram-Borus, in her discussion of multicultural considerations, reminds us that *all* group interventions are ecological interventions in that their impact reaches beyond the group room and the school, into various domains of students' lives. Further, group interventions cannot ignore forces outside the classroom, and therefore cannot be prescriptive without being contextual. This places sophisticated demands on service providers, as well as requirements to be knowledgeable about cultures, flexible, and remain in communication with students' caregivers and other service providers both inside and outside of the school.

These considerations suggest that support is needed by professionals to carry out and sustain high quality group interventions, and this topic is addressed in this volume as well (cf. Robinson & Elias). Involvement in group-based approaches may represent a relatively new focus of practice for many readers. Reading the professional literature and obtaining formal training are two valuable sources of assistance, but, as Robinson and Elias discuss, there is much benefit to be derived from setting up a supportive collegial structure within schools in which group interventions are being implemented. Further, there is benefit in obtaining support and supervision from colleagues who might be located in various settings. Peer-mediated learning experiences (e.g., peer support groups, peer supervision, peer review) refers to a small group of professionals with common interests who meet together regularly to learn from one another and solve work-related problems. These activities occur within the context of a collaborative, supportive atmosphere, involve group problem solving and the provision of critical feedback, and supplement traditional clinical supervision (Robinson & Elias, this volume; Zins, Ponti, & Murphy, 1993). These approaches to professional development show great promise as a means of enhancing the skills of special services providers (Zins, Wess, & Murphy, 1987) and of providing ways to allow interventions to evolve as they are tested in cultural contexts and with student populations different from those in which they may have been developed and validated.

ACKNOWLEDGEMENTS

We would like to sincerely thank each of the authors who joined us in creating this informative volume, and who so effectively shared their extensive expertise. Additional information about many of the programs is cited within the articles, and we encourage readers to seek out and review this detailed material. We extend appreciation to Charles Maher for his support of our undertaking this volume and for his constant availability and feedback. Finally, we once again wish to gratefully acknowledge the continuous support and inspiration of our respective families: Charlene, Lauren, and Michael and Ryan, and Ellen, Sara, and Samara.

REFERENCES

Bauman, L., Stein, R.E.K., & Ireys, H.T. (1991). Reinventing fidelity: The transfer of social technology among settings. *American Journal of Community Psychology, 19*, 619-639.

Claiborn, C.D., Kerr, B.A., & Strong, S.R. (1990). Group interventions in the schools. In T.B. Gutkin & C.R. Reynolds (Eds.), *The handbook of school psychology* (2nd ed., pp. 703-732). New York: Wiley.

Elias, M.J.(Ed.) (1993). *Social decision making and life skills development in the middle school: Models for excellence.* Gaithersburg, MD: Aspen.

Elias, M.J., & Tobias, S.E. (1990). *Problem solving/decision making for social and academic success: A school-based approach.* Washington, DC: National Education Association.

Lippitt, G.L., Langseth, P., & Mossop, J. (1986). *Implementing organizational change.* San Francisco: Jossey-Bass.

Tuma, J. (1989). Mental health services for children: The state of the art. *American Psychologist, 44*, 188-199.

Zins, J.E., Ponti, C.R., & Murphy, J.J. (1992). Peer-mediated professional development groups for special services practitioners. *Special Services in the Schools, 6(3), 179-194.*

Zins, J.E., Wess, B.P., & Murphy, J.J. (1987, August). *Professional peer support groups: Current practices of school psychologists.* Paper presented at the annual meeting of the American Psychological Association, New York.

Overview of Group Interventions for Special Services Providers

Stewart Ehly

University of Iowa

SUMMARY. Group interventions with children appear to offer an economical and effective means of addressing the academic and social-emotional needs of children. The article provides an overview of issues to consider by special services providers as they review options for service. An array of factors affecting the planning and implementation of group interventions is reviewed. Available alternatives for group interventions and guidelines for selecting, implementing, and evaluating options are considered.

Special services providers such as mental health counselors, school psychologists, and school social workers are faced with an awesome set of challenges in today's schools. Now as seldom in the past, schools are striving to respond to the diverse problems brought into the schools by children (cf. Natriello, McDill, & Pallas, 1990). Problems in the home, troubles with law enforcement officials, drug use, suicide, and friction with peers are just a few of the difficulties that children and adolescents present to school staff. The individual

---

Address correspondence to: Dr. Stewart Ehly, N336 Lindquist Center, University of Iowa, P.O. Box 2596, Iowa City, IA 52244.

[Haworth co-indexing entry note]: "Overview of Group Interventions for Special Services Providers." Ehly, Stewart. Co-published simultaneously in *Special Services in the Schools* (The Haworth Press, Inc.) Vol. 8, No. 1, 1993, pp. 9-38; and: *Promoting Student Success Through Group Interventions* (ed: Joseph E. Zins, and Maurice J. Elias) The Haworth Press, Inc., 1993, pp. 9-38. Multiple copies of this article/chapter may be purchased from The Haworth Document Delivery Center [1-800-3-HAWORTH; 9:00 a.m. - 5:00 p.m. (EST)].

administrator and classroom teacher face added concerns from the public about educational programs: articles on the failure of schools to prepare students for the responsibilities of adulthood are a common feature in the popular media.

Educators are on the front line working with children and adolescents. Yet few teachers would view their core responsibilities to include addressing every problem listed above. Instead, schools rely on community-based and in-house services, provided by special services providers, to extend remedial and preventive interventions to students. As Skrtic (1991b) argues, the services that are offered to children and their families involve assumptions, often untested, about what works best within the educational system. Children are served by special education and other programs which operate under important assumptions supporting individualized attention and the provision of services in a least restrictive environment. Available evidence suggests that group interventions could be used in addition to individualized services to expand the overall network of services available in the schools.

This introductory article examines, from several perspectives, the merits of group interventions with school-aged children. Subsequent articles feature a number of alternatives that can be used in group arrangements, with great success, to assist children and adolescents. In an introductory article, the author has the luxury of expanding the boundaries of discussion beyond those required to address an individual intervention option. Indeed, the potential array of group interventions available for use by special services providers greatly exceeds the limits of a single issue of any journal. For that reason, this paper reflects on several factors that influence the availability of group interventions within schools, as well as a rationale by which special services providers could argue for the expanded application of the described options.

The following topics are addressed within this paper:

a. The role of service providers in supporting the classroom teacher
b. Models of service within school settings
c. Traditional services via counseling and consultation
d. Group intervention options

e. Factors affecting professional decision making
   School characteristics
   Client characteristics
   Acceptability
   Treatment integrity
   Effectiveness
   Costs
f. General issues in evaluation
g. Professional development issues

The merits of any intervention reside in the ultimate benefits derived by the client. While urging the consideration of appropriate interventions within a school setting, the special services provider remains cognizant of the realities (read *politics*) of the setting. With that point in mind, let us begin with an exploration of the complex state of today's schools and the need and demand for interventions that support the work of the classroom teacher.

THE SPECIAL SERVICES PROVIDER AND THE CLASSROOM TEACHER

Today, the general public considers schools to be in crisis. Annual polls conducted by Phi Delta Kappa and the Gallup organization (Elam, Rose, & Gallup, 1991) attest to a consensus that schools are in disarray, children are in danger of not learning (if not in actual physical danger while attending school), and teachers are poorly prepared for the diversity of children found in many schools. Of great (if not ironic) interest in the survey data is the general satisfaction of parents with the schools that their children attend. The opinion of many parents is that although their local schools are doing fine, other school districts are struggling, other children's teachers are inadequately prepared, and other principals have lost control of the academic process within schools.

To dismiss such opinions as nay saying based on inadequate or inaccurate data is to miss the point of similar surveys–parents are frustrated, if not frightened, by what they see as the deteriorating state of American education. Authors such as Cuban (1990) have documented that concerns about schools are long-standing. Parents for more than a century have voiced dissatisfaction with the quality and outcomes of the educational enterprise. For only a portion of those 100 years schools have been served by an array of support professionals, such as counselors, social workers, and school psychologists. Today, school professionals come well prepared for their responsibilities (see, for example, Bardon's 1989 description of the skills offered by school psychologists). Yet with the availability of support, schools continue to struggle in their mission to serve all children.

Cuban (1990) is not the first to note the cyclical nature of demands to reform schools. Perkinson (1968), writing initially on the impact on schools of Lyndon Johnson's Great Society [and in a revised 1977 edition on reforms during the early 1970s], argued that Americans always have expected more than "book learning" to occur in public schools. Expectations that the teacher attend to more than reading, writing, and arithmetic have been present for decades. Yet with every demand placed on schools to address a societal concern (producing reforms in the mission of schools or expectations of teachers), little evidence exists to suggest that schools are the most viable vehicle or the best environment within which to affect any thing other than the education of children. Sarason (1971, 1982) is another recent voice challenging the assumptions under which schools operate and, more recently, by which they are being reformed to address problems of process and outcome (Sarason, 1990).

The evidence that our schools are straining to meet community expectations is available from a number of sources. In the most recent report by The National Assessment of Educational Progress (Mullis, Owen, & Phillips, 1990), an interesting conclusion emerges: schools today are producing students roughly equivalent in skills to the graduates of 20 years ago. Yet the public's consensus in 1992 about the skills necessary to succeed in the world of the 21st century does not match the perceptions of parents in the early 1970s. Goodlad (1990), for example, in his Study of the Education of Educators, proposes that schools and their teachers must be ready to meet the needs of children using strategies and tactics that emerge from the best available evidence about children, the learning process, and the means by which schools, as organizations, can be structured to provide an optimum environment for the multiple responsibilities of education.

Milofsky (1986) believes that educators share with their support service colleagues problems in mastering the demands created by the expectations of clients and the service institution: (1) undermanning–too few professionals are available to confront the total demand for services. In a closely related problem, professionals, by their success over the years, have heightened expectations for service, further straining the system; (2) undersupport–low pay, chronic shortages of support, and increases in responsibility add to the strain on professionals; (3) client acceptance–the priorities of children and their parents may not match those of the school and the service professional. The greatest challenge to the professional may involve convincing the client or family to assume the values or beliefs of the service organization; (4) imperfection of technologies–the options available to practitioners are not foolproof or guaranteed to work. Clients, in approaching the school, may present problems with few indications of the best way to proceed using existing school services; and (5) indivisibility of work–teachers and support professionals have varying degrees of autonomy to make important decisions about clients.

Poor services provided by a single professional or single school reflect on the overall quality of the service environment, schools, because of their focus on children and adolescents, are held to high standards for the custodial care of students. Teachers work informally as well as formally to support each other so that students are protected and assured an educational program that works in the interests of students.

Thus, the professional who works in schools, whether teacher, administrator, office staff, or special services provider proceeds toward goals that reflect institutional priorities. The mixture of services offered to children is founded on demands of the regular classroom, with special education alternatives built to reflect linkages to the regular class experience. Whether the mixture of services to children with special needs has been of ultimate benefit can be challenged (see Skrtic, 1991a; Milofsky, 1990). The premise for the remainder of this article is that special services providers can provide input to teachers and direct services to children to improve the quality of the educational experience. Special services providers have been and will continue to be crucial agents in structuring, delivering, and evaluating interventions with children. And, finally, the emphasis on group interventions evident within this special issue highlights viable strategies for improving the lives of children and the realities of life in classrooms.

An important consideration affecting our understanding of the merits of school programs centers on the quality of information that we have to guide our decisions. Research on the relative merits of program options is limited. Compounding the difficulty is the lack of evidence on the validity of various options with children of differing capabilities. We have few firm conclusions regarding the influence of gender, SES, or cultural and linguistic variations on the outcomes of interventions.

Multicultural Issues

Graham (1992), in a review of published research on African Americans in selected journals published by the American Psychological Association, found limited evidence that mainstream journals are publishing research on interventions with non-middle class or non-white populations. Graham argues that psychology must not "allow ethnic minorities to remain so marginalized in mainstream research" (p. 638). The paucity of information on representative groups of students within public schools may hinder our ability to select services that are valid for targeted children.

To guide the decisions of special services providers, the literature on cross-cultural interventions and multicultural awareness may offer direction. Pedersen (1988) argued that traditional forms of counseling provided to students rest on assumptions that are shared by only a small segment of the world's population. Within American society, such services worked best for members of the majority group, not students from linguistic or cultural minorities. Citing several sources, Pedersen believes that mental health services are biased toward the individual rather than the group (whether the family or the classroom). In addition, he believes that professionals have difficulty recognizing that their perceptions and actions reflect one system of cultural values, thus impairing their ability to perceive and understand the values of others.

Sue (1981) has written on the culturally effective counselor. Such practitioners are able to recognize their own values and assumptions, are aware that cultural factors may affect the counseling process, understand the social and political forces that affect the attitudes of minorities, and are skilled in establishing rapport and applying techniques from a variety of theoretical orientations. Skilled special services providers are not necessarily members of the same linguistic or cultural groups as the student; Atkinson (1983) suggested that minority students are not better served by minority rather than white counselors. Pedersen (1988) provides one perspective for approaching the issue of multicultural interventions: "it would be a serious mistake to assume that all members of a particular ethnic group take the same perspective on every issue, problem, or event. The differences of age, sex, life style, socioeconomic status, and a long list of variables in addition to ethnicity and nationality influence each individual's cultural perspective"(p. 102). Recognizing and appreciating the diversity represented within every child can help us to approach each intervention free of stereotypes and misguided notions on how best to serve children.

Sue and Sue (1990) encouraged all practitioners to become skilled in serving clients from all cultural groups. The authors propose that to become culturally skilled, the service provider must recognize that acquiring such skills is an active, ongoing, and never ending process, one that considers both the complexity of clients and the limitations of one's personal beliefs and perceptions.

MODELS OF SERVICE TO CLIENTS WITHIN THE SCHOOL

The services offered by support professionals within schools can be classified along four major dimensions, as suggested by Meyers, Parsons, and Martin (1979):

1. Direct services to children–the special services provider works with a child (or children) to offer support, counseling, training, or any other intervention considered appropriate;
2. Indirect services to children–by consulting with the classroom teacher, the professional assists in targeting areas of a child's functioning that will be addressed within an intervention;

3. Direct services to teachers–classroom teachers are assisted directly by counseling and other forms of support that improve their abilities to function within the classroom (see Caplan, 1970, for an extended rationale for direct services to help seekers);
4. Services at the system level–always an important form of intervention, the professional can work with system administrators to provide broadly focussed services that will affect groups of teachers (or other targeted staff). System change can be organization wide or directed at specific subsystems within the school district.

Each option can be pursued with success, but the selection of any single option will reflect the priorities of the help seeker, the help provider's perceptions of what will be viable given the presenting issues, and the organization's priorities for the use of the special services provider. Even the most highly skilled professional will be frustrated if s/he is unable, because of organization policies and expectations, to apply "best practices" in the service of clients.

Many special services providers are employed for the express purpose of working with children, especially children with needs that challenge the competencies of the regular classroom teacher. Several recent writers have urged that school-based professionals would better serve children if the adults who work with children (e.g., teachers and parents) were given top priority for service. Arguments favoring expanded services to teachers and parents can be stated in a systems' framework. Specifically, adults have important responsibilities for the sustenance, education, and custodial care of children. Children grow up within important systems–the family and the school. Children are better served if instead of directing our energies at changing the child, we consider the entire system within which the child operates and assist all participants in that system to collaborate to meet identified goals.

Conoley (1989), for example, has argued that theory and research on services to clients have evolved to a point at which the needs of any individual cannot be separated from those of the broader system within which the client operates. She calls for greater use of nontraditional forms of service to children and adults, with the intent of addressing behaviors that are adversely affecting the functioning of individuals and their families.

In a separate vein, Gutkin and Conoley (1990) call for a reconceptualization of the profession of school psychology, proposing a shift that would favor indirect services (e.g., consultation) to children and their families. Given that special services providers operate to help children through involvement with important adults in the children's lives, professionals must become more successful in helping caregivers to acquire the skills and attitudes necessary to be more successful with childrearing and education responsibilities. The authors note that professionals need a focus "that is significantly more adult-centered than current practice if there is to be any real hope of attaining consistent positive change for children" (p. 211).

Professionals have several potential tools for viewing the problems of children within systems, including the extensive literature from marriage and family therapy. Green (1988) represents one of several valuable perspectives by which system variables can be assessed to provide basic data on interactions within families, and, by extension, other systems.

The special services provider may feel unprepared to integrate recent practices and findings reflected in the latest literature on system models. As the array of services within schools shifts to absorb attempts at reform (whether implemented by the public or the professional community), practitioners can collaborate with researchers to evaluate and study the impact of new interventions. Huberman (1990), in considering the gap between research and practice, argues that both researchers and practitioners can assume responsibility for collaboration, if the goal is to infuse knowledge from controlled studies into the service arena.

TRADITIONAL SERVICES USING COUNSELING AND CONSULTATION

Counseling and consultation are attractive intervention choices for special services providers. Counseling of students offers the alternative of working individually with children or with groups of students experiencing common difficulties within school, the home, or the community. Consultation, though used within schools more often as a means to assist a teacher with a single child, also allows for service to be provided for groups of children. In the following paragraphs details are offered on the use of counseling and consultation.

Counseling

Counseling in groups is a common way of addressing the affective needs of children. The wealth of theories within the counseling and psychotherapy literature provides special services providers with valuable information for planning interventions (Prout & Brown, 1983). Ehly and Dustin (1989) review three theories of counseling (Rogerian, Adlerian, behavioral) that vary in their goals for intervention.

Rogerian groups focus on intrapersonal awareness, leading group members to explore their feelings and perceptions about themselves. Members interact and reveal personal insights. Group leaders help the group to set goals and to foster openness.

Adlerian groups work towards goals of self-awareness, and emphasize members' understanding of thinking and behavior. Children are taught to reflect on their goals and how their behavior relates to their motives, values, and beliefs. Commonly cited goals within the Adlerian perspective include the need for attention, the desire for power, the need for revenge, and a need to display helplessness (Corsini, 1984).

Behavioral groups consider specific goals for change. Students are trained to define behaviors that will be changed and to complete a commitment (often a contract) for change with the group leader or members. When a goal for change is met, the group may be involved in providing reinforcement for the target student.

The usefulness of a theoretical approach will depend on the practitioner's reactions to the following questions:

1. Does the special services provider understand the theory, its key terms and constructs?
2. Are interventions being considered for use with students influenced by the theoretical assumptions within a specific approach?
3. Are the goals espoused within a theoretical orientation consis-

tent with the goals of the service profession and service setting?
4. Can the special services provider offer techniques consistent with the approach (i.e., does the practitioner have prerequisite skills)?
5. Does the theory provide a means to evaluate progress and outcomes? (Ehly & Dustin, 1989)

All group counseling options require the involvement of a skilled leader who is available to guide students as needed, and to serve as a model of specific behaviors. For example, a leader who expects group members to communicate with each other and to allow individual members to be heard without interruption must be able to help the group understand the importance of expected behaviors and to assist members to engage in productive interpersonal exchanges.

Group counseling, with its emphasis on working with several students at one time, offers a seemingly efficient way to intervene with students. Yet as many readers will understand, developing an environment within which children can work in groups carries its own demands on the leader's time and energies. For example, in schools that offer group counseling to students considered at risk of school failure, the tasks of recruiting and maintaining group-membership, let alone guiding members toward productive use of the counseling sessions, can represent challenges to the special services provider.

The leader of group counseling is faced with important responsibilities in moving discussion towards closure. Leaders require skills in (1) direct questions (being able to query individual members and the entire group) that provide structure to discussion, probes for clarification, requests for expanded information, and other priorities for group process; (2) focusing comments (statements that challenge members to reflect on group functioning); and (3) process comments (reflections by the leader in which s/he offers reactions on how the group is functioning or requests feedback of same) that further guide members to consider the purposes and proceedings of the group (Ehly & Dustin, 1989).

The skilled group counseling leader draws on important communication techniques that allow for the expression and discussion of affect. Techniques that can be used by the leader include the following:

1. Acknowledging feelings expressed by the group member(s) (a statement that recognizes the content or expression of an emotion, as delivered by the student);
2. Restating the feeling (repeating a student's statement of feeling, a technique that extends acknowledgment and empathy);
3. Paraphrasing a feeling (offering a condensed version of a student's expression of affect, at times substituting a synonym for the affective language used by the child);
4. Adding to feelings (augmenting, emphasizing, or accentuating the affective language expressed by the student or the entire group, challenging the member(s) to clarify the extent or characteristics of experienced feelings);
5. Asking for feelings (directing questions about feelings to the student or the entire group);
6. Drawing in other members (querying members about feelings being expressed by a particular student); and
7. Self-disclosing feelings (leader expressing feelings and leading group to react and express their own feelings) (Ehly & Dustin, 1989).

Successful leaders similarly will be prepared to deal with the silence of individual members and the entire group, defensiveness or resistance of members, and hostility or disruption that affects the group's structure or process. Each of these situations can occur no matter what issue is being pursued by group members.

Ehly and Dustin (1989) list common topics discussed within school-aged counseling groups. At the elementary school-level, attitudes and behaviors towards others (including peers, siblings, parents, other adults) often are considered. Issues of meeting the challenges of the transition to middle or junior high school may be a target for older students at this level.

By middle/junior high, student groups deal with peer relations, attitudes and behaviors with members of the opposite sex, responses to academic situations, and relations with parents. Group counseling leaders explore with members reasons for involvement in the group and what each member can expect to learn through participation.

Senior high students participate in counseling groups that explore the same themes as do younger students, with added topics of planning for the future (whether in terms of post-secondary education or career-related issues) as part of the agenda for group sessions. At any of the age levels, a narrow focus on specific conditions having an impact on the child can become the leader's motive for structuring sessions. For example, a group can be developed around issues of divorce within the students' families, substance use/abuse by the students or their peers (even siblings), and other topics (e.g., suicide, eating disorders, etc.) that affect a defined subsection of students being served by the school professional.

Group counseling of students can be offered by any of the special services providers within a system. Counselors, school psychologists, and social workers are three professional groups experienced with the requirements of effective group approaches. Literature on group counseling, with its extensive consideration of issues relating to the theory, research, and practice of counseling, is available for applications by special services providers (Patterson, 1988).

Consultation

The evolution of the literature on consultation has been rapid since the 1970 classic text by Caplan, *The Theory and Practice of Mental Health Consultation.* Reports and studies of consultation now number in the thousands. The early work of Caplan, while offering extended detail on the use of consultation techniques to effect change of an individual client, also elaborated on techniques to address group or system-level targets for change.

The abundant research inspired by Bergan's (1977) text on behavioral consultation typically considers the individual client as the focus for change. A close reading of Bergan, especially his more recent work with Kratochwill (Bergan & Kratochwill, 1990; Kratochwill & Bergan, 1990), clarifies the potential utility of applying behavioral techniques to the planning and implementation of group-level goals for change. Indeed, Bergan, throughout his writing, has argued that his model for consultation is a vehicle by which any version of a behavioral intervention can be delivered to a consultee (help seeker).

Other models of consultation take into account the fact that help seekers operate in environments that can contain multiple actors and conditions that must be considered prior to intervention planning. Assessment of environmental conditions is a prerequisite to developing the details of an intervention plan. Zins, Curtis, Graden, and Ponti (1988) offer a system-level approach to consultation interventions that can be adapted to address problems being experienced by groups of students. The Zins et al. text is one of the few discussions of system-level change via consultation within school settings (in contrast, numerous accounts of system-level change exist in the literature from business and industry; see French & Bell, 1990).

The many consultation approaches practiced in schools follow a common course toward problem solving; indeed, problem-solving strategies that have evolved from any theoretical orientation can be integrated into a consultation framework. Zins and Ponti (1990) list four critical stages or elements to consultation relationships:

1. Establishment of the relationship: at entry, the consultant works to establish rapport, build trust, understand the consultee's system and work situation. Gallessich (1982) proposed that entry could be divided into two dimensions: physical and psychological. The latter may require extended contact between consultant and consultee before problem-solving proceeds with efficiency and effectiveness;
2. Problem identification: the external consultant (i.e., one from outside of the consultee's system) unfamiliar with the requirements of the consultee's situation has a great deal to learn before achieving clarification on the presenting problem and its context. The internal consultant, though embedded within the consultee's organization, does not always work at an advantage within the problem identification phase. All consultants work to define the presenting problem, gather information (e.g., data) on characteristics of the problem, identify conditions that may contribute to the problem or to a solution for the

consultee, and survey resources (human and material) that can be mobilized to develop an intervention;

3. Intervention development and refinement: acting on information generated within #2, the consultant and consultee collaborate to explore potential interventions addressed at the defined problem. Eventual agreement on the single best approach to intervention can reflect limitations of resources (e.g., time, energy, materials) or a commitment to action built on consensus between the two parties. The plan is usually implemented by the consultee, who maintains ultimate responsibility for all aspects of the intervention;
4. Implementation, evaluation, follow-up: consultation models are structured so that problem-solving efforts can be modified and refocused at any stage of application. During plan implementation, for example, the consultee may perceive that intervention procedures do not reflect a critical characteristic of the environment or client (e.g., the student is out-of-seat frequently). The collaborators can pause in their efforts to assess and adjust planned procedures. In-progress and final outcome indicators of success are built into intervention plans. Consideration for generalizing or maintaining procedures can become part of follow-up efforts with the consultee (Zins & Ponti, 1990).

While the above recommendations suggest that consultation planning is a strictly rational process, one that can be built on purely objective data, Schön (1983) suggests that there are factors that significantly influence the direction and outcomes of planning. Schön's concept of *problem setting* relates to the complexity of understanding critical dimensions of the change process and the environment within which change occurs.

Schön offers the example of a community which elects to build a bridge across a body of water. Where does the bridge get built? The process of determining the best possible site, structure, and use of the bridge will reflect a dizzying array of factors (e.g., engineering, economic, environmental, etc.) that render the characterization of a single "best" solution impossible. Relating the concept of problem setting to consultation, the consultant and consultee can produce any of an infinite number of "best" interventions. The consultant who recognizes the inherent subjectivity of the change process will have a realistic grasp of the wealth of possibilities to effect an intervention.

Consultation addressed at problems identified as affecting a group of students will involve special services providers and educators in planning that can integrate any of the group interventions considered below. To re-state an earlier point, consultation represents a collection of communication techniques, strategies and tactics that assist the help seeker to approach planning. The content of the intervention plans can include activities reflecting any theoretical or practical approach.

GROUP INTERVENTIONS

The other articles in this issue represent several of the alternatives available for group interventions within schools. All utilize the resources and skills of special services providers. Any school-aged child could become involved in and benefit from these options, although many schools identify sub-groups of the school population (e.g., students in special education, "at-risk" students) for priority status for service.

Students in academic difficulty are routinely served by special education-funded programs. Consistent with federal and state mandates, children are provided with services that take into account the best interests of each student. Theoretical orientation of the special services provider will influence how the practitioner evaluates data on the student and determines an optimal plan of intervention (see D'Amato & Rothlisberg, 1992).

The abundance of information on school-based intervention includes details on strategies that can address the cognitive, social-emotional, physical, and behavioral status of any student, whether served by special education, other remedial programs, or the general education teacher. Maher and Zins (1987) offer a survey of alternatives by which psychoeducational interventions can be structured. Several of the contributors to their volume recognize that group interventions are possible, depending on the focus of the planned strategies, goals for each participant, and the requirements of individual students. Such interventions can be an important element of the service provider's work with children prior to referral to special programs.

Miller and Peterson (1987), for example, explore the popular area of peer-mediated interventions. Involving students in cooperative learning ventures, peer tutoring, and peer counseling has proceeded for many years (Ehly & Dustin, 1989; Ehly & Larsen, 1980; Johnson & Johnson, 1978). Miller and Peterson (1987) provide a useful summary of several cooperative learning ventures that have been implemented with success. Activities include Student Teams, Jigsaw, Group Investigation, and related group-oriented procedures. Documentation of the merits of cooperative learning has been extensive (Johnson, Maruyama, Johnson, Nelson, & Skon, 1981), though some researchers have challenged areas of assumed benefits (Slavin, 1983).

Peer tutoring has been shown to produce useful gains in children's academic performance, although claims for gains in affective areas are less consistently demonstrated (Cohen, Kulik, & Kulik, 1982). Ehly and Larsen (1980) examined the broad array of programs implemented under the rubric of peer tutoring, finding same-age (true peer) and cross-age programs with almost every possible combination of children. Peer tutoring programs, while generally focused on the learning needs of individual tutees, can involve large groups of students in a single school or entire school district. Melaragno (1976) proposed that whole schools can become involved in tutorial activities, with every child serving as tutor and tutee at several points during the school week.

Peer counseling, which involves training students to work with classmates, is provided in many school districts. Involvement of children with peers provides an important service to individual students, but the actual preparation of peer helpers to assist groups of students seldom is documented (Ehly & Dustin, 1989). The skills identified above as critical to the effectiveness of special services providers apply similarly to peer counselors working to advise or comfort classmates. Readers interested in additional information on implementing peer counseling programs will appreciate recent articles by de Rosenroll and Dey (1990), Garner, Martin, and Martin (1989), and Morey, Miller, Fulton, Rosen, and Daly (1989).

The management of behavior within the classroom often is

framed as a group-level concern. Phillips (1980), in considering several options for classroom interventions addressing student behavior, recognized that seldom do identified problem behaviors exist independent of the learning environment, the teacher, and peers. Behavior change strategies commonly involve participation of peers, including use of groups of peers as targets for intervention activities. The interested reader can consult Strain's (1981) *The Utilization of Classroom Peers as Behavior Change Agents* for extensive information on means by which peers can become involved in interventions (individual or group).

The intervention programs being developed for so-called "at-risk" students often define these students as falling outside of the catchment areas of special education. Programs designed to serve at-risk students have met with varying degrees of success. Slavin, Karweit, and Madden (1989) concluded the following after completing a comprehensive review of school programs for high-risk students:

1. The setting within which remedial services are provided makes little difference to the ultimate success of the program and its impact on the student. What does matter is the quality of the programs implemented in the setting;
2. Prevention and early intervention are much more promising than waiting for difficulties in learning to accumulate before providing remedial services. Early intervention works and is needed within schools;
3. Effective classroom and pullout programs for students at risk tend to provide individualized instruction. They often assist a student to progress through a structured hierarchy of skills while adapting instructional materials and strategies;
4. Early intervention programs (preschool/extended kindergarten) can contribute to the cognitive and social development of children from low SES backgrounds;
5. Remedial services often are integrated poorly with regular education programs and burden the student with the responsibility of accommodating very different approaches;
6. Teacher behaviors associated with successful services to at-risk children are similar to behaviors found to be effective with all students.

Schools that target prevention of at-risk behaviors or address specific risk factors can provide services in several areas. *Primary prevention* allows for large numbers of students to be exposed to information on and discussion of issues related to growth and development. A school, for example, might provide training to all students on self-esteem and encourage children to think and act as individuals. Planned activities are developed to inoculate students from the full impact of risk factors within the environment.

Secondary prevention targets students exposed to significant levels of stress or disruption, offering guidance and skill training to assist each student to avoid future difficulties. A school might offer group counseling to students struggling with academic classes, in an effort to keep students enrolled and progressing in school.

Tertiary prevention programs address problems of students who have engaged already in high-risk behaviors and are being assisted toward participation in more conventional patterns of behavior. A school can cooperate with a community agency to operate a follow-through program for adolescent drug offenders upon their return from a treatment facility.

All levels of prevention can be offered within a community, even within a single agency (e.g., school) within that community (Auerbach & Stolberg, 1986). The current literature, however, cannot tell educators the best strategy by which each student can be motivated, inspired, educated, and retained in school until graduation. Although many programs have emerged to serve students experiencing difficulty, much remains to be developed, implemented, and evaluated.

The articles in this special issue are one attempt to expand awareness and knowledge about an important form of intervention: group-oriented approaches. Given the success of other forms of peer involvement activities, the interventions hold promise for educators in general and specialized school programs. Factors that affect the creation, application, and impact of group interventions now can be explored.

FACTORS AFFECTING DECISION MAKING ON INTERVENTIONS

Evidence from many settings has accumulated on variables that can play a major role in shaping the implementation and consequences of an intervention. Special services providers can make decisions with reference to a client's characteristics, classroom environment, characteristics of the intervention itself (acceptability, efficacy, cost-effectiveness), and the ethics of the practitioner-client relationship (see section on Professional Development).

Client characteristics are important within several psychological perspectives on intervention planning (D'Amato & Rothlisberg, 1992). In considering possibilities for group interventions, a preference to serve several clients with similar or related problems is necessary (Ehly & Dustin, 1989). While heterogeneous groupings are possible on dimensions such as gender, homogeneity is introduced in terms of client presenting problems or goals for behavior change.

The *environment* within which a group of students works, whether a formal classroom or other activity area, is considered a priority for assessment by practitioners of behavioral and ecological interventions. Conoley and Haynes (1992), in presenting the ecological approach, identify three critical elements to interventions: (1) children are considered to be inseparable parts of the targeted social system (as are teachers and other adults within the classroom); (2) disturbance is assumed to reflect the system rather than a disease or problem located within a child. The environment can be structured in ways that influence participant (children and adults) behaviors; and (3) problems are cast as a "failure of match between child and system" (p. 180). The special services provider works to understand both the abilities of the child and the demands or expectations of the environment. Practitioners recognize that children can and do behave very differently across settings, time, and with different adults present.

Characteristics of the intervention have come under intense scrutiny within the literature. Reynolds, Gutkin, Elliott, and Witt (1984) identified four important dimensions to consider when faced with a choice of interventions. The authors discuss acceptability, effectiveness, cost, and treatment integrity. In the real world, consideration of each of these factors cannot occur independently of the others.

Treatment acceptability has received extensive attention in the past few years. Elliott (1988), Reimers, Wacker, and Koeppl (1987), and Witt and Elliott (1985) serve as examples of the analogue and "live" applications of acceptability ratings that are possible with clients. The Reimers et al. (1987) review found that the acceptability of an intervention relates to implementation by clients and to eventual outcomes. In brief, if a child and the parents find a proposed intervention to be acceptable, the child and parents are more likely to implement and derive benefits from that intervention than will be the case if they do not consider the recommended procedure acceptable.

Reynolds et al. (1984) noted that people are relatively consistent in deciding whether a treatment is acceptable. Relevant dimensions of the proposed intervention are (1) the seeming appropriateness of the intervention to the given problem; (2) the perceived fairness and intrusiveness of recommendations; and (3) the degree to which the treatment matches the client's beliefs concerning what an acceptable intervention should be.

The available research on treatment acceptability provides an interesting array of factors to consider when deciding how to match a client to an intervention. Missing from the literature on acceptability, however, is detailed consideration of interventions targeted at group arrangements.

Effectiveness of a given intervention can be determined, in part, by standard means of evaluation. As evidence on the use of a specific procedure accumulates, practitioners develop greater confidence in the applicability of an intervention for a given problem or concern. Reynolds et al. (1984) stated what may seem obvious to many special services providers: "We can not specify *in advance* whether a treatment will be effective for a given problem" (p. 216). Given the truth of that statement, the practitioner must be informed by the available evidence (read *research*) on an intervention and remain cautious in fostering expectations. Recommendations toward caution are in line with Schön's (1983) admonition to avoid casting oneself as an expert capable of solving all problems. To paraphrase his suggestion, the professional can work to convince a help seeker that s/he is a reasonable alternative to tackling a problem without any assistance.

Effectiveness can be determined at several points of an intervention. The practitioner attempts to verify that intervention procedures are being implemented as planned (see below) while collecting information/data on the client's behavior. Effectiveness can be investigated by following up on the client and soliciting input from the teacher or other referral sources. Without data, the special services provider will be in no position to argue convincingly that an intervention produced a desired effect.

Cost of an intervention enters into the determination of what will be recommended. The cost of special education, for example, has had a profound effect on the services created and the number of children served (Skrtic, 1991a). Although the visible indicators of an intervention's cost can be calculated in dollars, the impact of an intervention on the child's and teacher's time and energy are other important dimensions that must be considered during planning. A peer tutoring program that involves several students, for example, will require a great deal of teacher time to organize, let alone materials that can strain the school's budget. Not to be ignored are the tradeoffs for participants. What do students gain through their participation? What do they lose by being diverted from other instructional activities?

Finally, *treatment integrity* must be monitored to insure that planned procedures are being implemented as scheduled. Special services providers, in recommending an intervention to a teacher, can improve treatment integrity by preparing the teacher for every step and required action over the course of the intervention. Advance planning alerts the practitioner and the teacher to each expectation for the affected children and the adults responsible for portions of an intervention strategy.

Taken together, the four dimensions in considering alternative treatments can help school professionals make appropriate intervention choices. By monitoring implementation of a choice and by evaluating outcomes, the practitioner can help teachers learn to address the challenges and complexities of managing their classrooms.

EVALUATION OF INTERVENTIONS

Good practice includes gathering data on the effects of an intervention, no matter how limited the attempt at changing a child's behavior. Data can assist the professional to convince a parent, teacher, or school administrator that something indeed has occurred (or failed to occur) for the student. Data that accurately reflect the child's behavior can inform the practitioner on when to shift strategy and tactics.

When engaging in a group intervention, the importance of evaluation is magnified. Information on process and outcomes can be collected by students, educators, or service providers, and then be perused to determine the need for adjustments or revision of overall strategy. Reppucci and Haugaard (1989) argue that very few potentially worthy programs implement a sufficiently rigorous or comprehensive evaluation component to assess the true impact of their programs. Without valid evidence of the impact of interventions, programs have difficulty convincing consumers and funding sources that children are being helped.

Student progress in a group intervention can be monitored by considering:

1. Student satisfaction with the activities;
2. Training of students in ways they can support each other during group activities. If peer leaders are used, training can occur prior to activities and establish criteria for conduct in the leader role;
3. Faculty and special services provider understanding of the intervention plan. All participants must understand what will be occurring, who is responsible for each activity, and the time frame within which activities will occur;
4. Record keeping by participants. Documentation is aided when participants share responsibility for confirming the process and products of interventions; and
5. Agreement on what constitutes evidence of progress and success. When all participants are aware of expectations, goals, and measures of progress and outcomes, work can proceed with informed collaboration.

The larger issue of the effectiveness of group approaches within the total service plan within a school requires consideration of additional factors;

1. The role of group interventions in the total plan;
2. The cost, on a per-pupil basis, of each intervention option;

3. The priority attached to each option by parents, students, administrators, educators, and special services providers; and
4. The satisfaction of the same groups with the products of each option.

Guidelines for effective evaluation of services fall outside the scope of this paper. Readers are advised to consider the following articles, and the means by which authors verified the process and products of their interventions. McConnell (1990) can be consulted for specific guidelines on the creation of evaluation plans.

ISSUES IN PROFESSIONAL DEVELOPMENT

Special services providers face daily challenges in their responsibilities to educators, parents, and students. The ethical professional recognizes that every client must receive the best possible service at the time of need (Bayles, 1981). Ethical codes provide structure to the practitioner by offering guidelines for the conduct of practice. Sockett (1990) notes that accountability (to consumers and to the profession) evolves from an ethical code of practice.

Ethical mandates inform practitioners in major education service professions (e.g., school psychology, school counseling) and are a topic of intense discussion among consumers of those services (Strike, 1990). Monitoring one's actions and reflecting on the ethical justification of one's words and actions represent important aspects of professional development. The process of reflection can be cast as a career-long process by which the individual remains open to knowledge and the refinement of skills. Schön (1987) recognizes that the skills central to reflection must be learned by every professional before they can become integrated into thoughts and actions.

One conclusion following reflection may be that the professional lacks the necessary expertise in selecting and implementing group interventions. Given the lack of detailed information on "best practices" in group interventions, a professional may conclude that s/he needs to review the existing literature, engage in small-scale research, or participate in continuing education training before feeling confident *and* competent in working with groups of students.

An important area of competency relates to factors involved in multicultural contact with students and parents. As noted earlier, the multiculturally competent practitioner is sensitive to personal limitations while engaging in services to students. Pedersen (1988) proposes the following goals for educators: (1) be familiar with the customs, language, and history of the cultures represented among students; (2) be able to locate information on students' cultures and understand the implications of cultural data on service planning; and (3) be competent in developing school activities that contribute to the academic and social development of every student. Many component skills and attitudes combine to affect the ultimate impact of the practitioner on students from linguistic and racial-ethnic minorities. The ethical special services provider remains open to information on students and maintains with all students the goal of providing the best possible service that addresses individual and collective needs.

CLOSING COMMENTS

This article has explored several issues relating to intervention planning and implementation. While the express focus on group-level intervention has been maintained throughout, it is recognized that special services providers face many more work-related decisions than whether or not to recommend or attempt a group intervention. The pressures of work within schools are intense and influence the timing and quality of recommendations. The practitioner committed to serving children already is aware of group interventions that work, and only needs the time and tools to develop programs.

The articles in this volume, and studies cited from the broader literature, represent important steps towards understanding how children can be served best within the schools. Group interventions are attractive to many educators and support professionals because all parties recognize that students seldom experience difficulties in isolation from their peers. Working with several students on an issue has intuitive appeal, if only for the savings of time and energy that seem apparent.

Yet what may appear at first to be obvious can be misleading, if not damaging to students. The group option for intervention is approached with recognition that individual children may not benefit in a group setting or may experience more immediate or longer-lasting gains when served one-to-one by the professional.

The author supports the attitude that special services providers always will work to enhance and refine their understanding of students and the means by which children are educated. Practitioners may be influenced by the latest trends in school reform, but ongoing responsibilities to students will keep professional sights on the short- and long-term consequences of services. Each special services provider adds to our knowledge base by attempting *and* evaluating interventions created in the best interests of children.

Selecting the "best" group intervention in a given situation will be influenced by such factors as

1. the urgency of the situation. In general, group approaches require more preparation time;
2. the goals of the school's special services program. Group interventions can be attractive components of a school's overall strategy for addressing student needs; and
3. the input of students, parents, and school staff. Services that appeal to the school and community's priorities and needs will be appealing to consumers, especially if outcomes can be documented and discussed.

Group interventions can be a strategy of choice, matching the interests of educators, special services providers, and the community served. A service plan that integrates individual and group approaches to interventions will be able to provide a broad range of programs that can address student needs.

REFERENCES

Atkinson, D. R. (1983). Ethnic similarity in counseling: A review of research. *Counseling Psychologist, 11*, 35-41.

Auerbach, S. M., & Stolberg, A. L. (Eds.). (1986). *Crisis intervention with children and families*. Washington: Hemisphere.

Bardon, J. I. (1989). The school psychologist as an applied educational psychologist. In R. C. D'Amato & R. S. Dean (Eds.), *The school psychologist in nontraditional settings* (pp. 1-32). Hillsdale, NJ: Erlbaum.

Bayles, M. D. (1981). *Professional ethics*. Belmont, CA: Wadsworth.

Bergan, J. R. (1977). *Behavioral consultation*. Columbus, OH: Charles E. Merrill.

Bergan, J. R., & Kratochwill, T. R. (1990). *Behavioral consultation and therapy*. New York: Plenum.

Caplan, G. (1970). *The theory and practice of mental health consultation*. New York: Basic Books.

Cohen, P. A., Kulik, J. A., & Kulik, C. C. (1982). Educational outcomes of tutoring: A meta-analysis of findings. *American Educational Research Journal, 19*, 237-248.

Conoley, J. C. (1989). The school psychologist as a community/family service provider. In R. C. D'Amato & R. S. Dean (Eds.), *The school psychologist in nontraditional settings: integrating clients, services, and settings* (pp. 33-65). Hillsdale, NJ: Erlbaum.

Conoley, J. C., & Haynes, G. (1992). An ecological approach to intervention. In R. C. D'Amato & B. A. Rothlisberg (Eds.), *Psychological perspectives on intervention. A case study approach to prescriptions for change* (pp. 177-189). New York: Longman.

Corsini, R. J. (1984). *Current psychotherapies* (3rd ed.). ltasca, IL: Peacock.

Cuban, L. (1990). Reforming again, again, and again. *Educational Researcher, 19*(1), 3-13.

D'Amato, R. C., & Rothlisberg, B. A. (Eds.).(1992). *Psychological perspectives on intervention. A case study approach to prescriptions for change*. New York: Longman.

de Rosenroll, D. A., & Dey, C. (1990). A centralized approach to training peer counselors: 3 years of progress. *The School Counselor, 37*, 304-312.

Ehly, S., & Dustin, R. (1989). *Individual and group counseling in schools*. New York: Guilford.

Ehly, S. W., & Larsen, S. C. (1980). *Peer tutoring for individualized instruction*. Boston: Allyn and Bacon.

Elam, S. M., Rose, L. C., & Gallup, A. M. (1991). The 23rd annual Gallup Poll of the public's attitudes toward the public schools. *Phi Delta Kappan, 73*(1), 41-56.

Elliott, S. N. (1988). Acceptability of behavioral treatments in educational settings. In J. C. Witt, S. N. Elliott, & F. M. Gresham (Eds.), *Handbook of behavior therapy in education* (pp. 121-150). New York: Plenum.

French, W. L., & Bell, C. H. (1990). *Organization development. Behavioral science interventions for organizations improvement* (4th ed.). Englewood Cliffs, NJ: Prentice-Hall.

Gallessich, J. (1982). *The profession and practice of consultation*. San Francisco: Jossey-Bass.

Garner, R., Martin, D., & Martin, M. (1989). The PALS program: A peer counseling training program for junior high school. *Elementary School Guidance & Counseling, 24*, 68-76.

Goodlad, J. I. (1990). Better teachers for our nation's schools. *Phi Delta Kappan, 73*(3), 185-194.

Graham, S. (1992). "Most of the subjects were white and middle class." Trends in published research on African Americans in selected APA journals, 1970-1989. *American Psychologist, 47*, 629-639.

Green, R. J. (1988). Impasse and change: A systemic/strategic view of the therapeutic system. *Journal of Marriage and Family Therapy, 14*, 383-395.

Gutkin, T. B., & Conoley, J. C. (1990). Reconceptualizing school psychology from a service delivery perspective: Implications for practice, training, and research. *Journal of School Psychology, 28*, 203-223.

Huberman, M. (1990). Linkage between researchers and practitioners: A qualitative study. *American Educational Research Journal, 27*, 363-391.

Johnson, D., & Johnson, R. (1978). Cooperative, competitive and individualistic learning. *Journal of Research and Development in Education, 12*(1), 3-15.

Johnson, D., Maruyama, G., Johnson, R., Nelson, D., & Skon, L. (1981). The effects of cooperative, competitive and individualistic goal structures on achievement: A meta-analysis. *Psychological Bulletin, 89*, 47-62.

Kratochwill, T. R., & Bergan, J. R. (1990). *Behavioral consultation in applied settings*. New York: Plenum.

Maher, C. A., & Zins, J. E. (Eds.). (1987). *Psychoeducational interventions in schools: Methods and procedures for enhancing student competence*. New York: Pergamon.

McConnell, S. R. (1990). Best practices in evaluating educational programs. In A. Thomas & J. Grimes (Eds.), *Best practices in school psychology II*, (pp. 353-370). Washington, DC: National Association of School Psychologists.

Melaragno, R. J. (1976). *Tutoring with students. A handbook for establishing tutorial programs in schools*. Englewood Cliffs, NJ: Educational Technology Publications.

Meyers, J., Parsons, R. D., & Martin, R. (1979). *Mental health consultation in the schools*. San Francisco: Jossey-Bass.

Miller, J. A., & Peterson. D. W. (1987). Peer-influenced academic interventions. In C. A. Maher & J. E. Zins (Eds.), *Psychoeducational interventions in schools. Methods and procedures for enhancing student competence* (pp. 81-100). New York: Pergamon.

Milofsky, C. D. (1986). Special education and social control. In J. G. Richardson (Ed.), *Handbook of theory and research for the sociology of education* (pp. 173-202). New York: Greenwood.

Morey, R. E., Miller, C. D., Fulton, R., Rosen, L. A., & Daly, J. L. (1989). Peer counseling: Students served, problems discussed, overall satisfaction, and perceived helpfulness. *The School Counselor, 37*, 137-143.

Mullis, I. V. S., Owen, E. H., & Phillips, G. W. (1990). *America's challenge: Accelerating academic achievement. A summary of findings from 20 years of NAEP*. Washington, DC: U. S. Department of Education.

Natriello, G., McDill, E. L., & Pallas, A. M. (1990). *Schooling disadvantaged children: Racing against catastrophe*. New York: Teachers College Press.

Patterson, C. H. (1986). *Theories of counseling and psychotherapy* (4th ed.). New York: Harper & Row.

Pedersen, P. (1988). *A handbook for developing multicultural awareness*. Alexandria, VA: American Association for Counseling and Development.

Perkinson, H. J. (1968; 1977). *The imperfect panacea: American faith in education*. New York: Random House.

Phillips, B. W. (Ed.) (1980). *Management of behavior in the classroom: A handbook of psychological strategies*. Los Angeles: Western Psychological Services.

Prout, H. T., & Brown, D. T. (Eds.). (1983). *Counseling and psychotherapy with children and adolescents: Theory and practice for school and clinic settings*. Tampa, FL: Mariner.

Reimers, T. M., Wacker, D. P., & Koeppl, G. (1987). Acceptability of behavioral interventions: A review of the literature. *School Psychology Review, 16*, 212-227.

Reppucci, N. D., & Haugaard, J. J. (1989). Prevention of child sexual abuse: Myth or reality. *American Psychologist, 44*, 1266-1275.

Reynolds, C. R., Gutkin, T. B., Elliott, S. N., & Witt, J. C. (1984). *School psychology: Essentials of theory and practice*. New York: Wiley.

Sarason, S. B. (1971; 1982). *The culture of the school and the problem of change*. Boston: Allyn and Bacon.

Sarason, S. B. (1990). *The predictable failure of educational reform*. San Francisco: Jossey-Bass.

Schön, D. A. (1983). *The reflective practitioner*. New York: Basic Books.

Schön, D. A. (1987). *Educating the reflective practitioner*. San Francisco: Jossey-Bass.

Skrtic, T. M. (1991 a). *Behind special education. A critical analysis of professional culture and school organization*. Denver: Love.

Skrtic, T. M. (1991 b). The special education paradox: Equity as the way to excellence. *Harvard Educational Review, 61*(2), 148-206.

Slavin, R. E. (1983). *Cooperative learning*. London: Longman.

Slavin, R. E., Karweit, N. L, & Madden, N. A. (1989). *Effective programs for students at risk*. Boston: Allyn and Bacon.

Sockett, H. (1990). Accountability, trust, and ethical codes of practice. In J. I. Goodlad, R. Soder & K. A. Sirotnik (Eds.), *The moral dimensions of teaching* (pp. 224-250). San Francisco: Jossey-Bass.

Strain, P. S. (Ed.). (1981). *The utilization of classroom peers as behavior change agents*. New York: Plenum.

Strike, K. A. (1990). The legal and moral responsibility of teachers. In J. I. Goodlad, R. Soder, & K. A. Sirotnik (Eds.), *The moral dimensions of teaching*. (pp. 188-223). San Francisco: Jossey-Bass.

Sue, D. W. (1981). *Counseling the culturally different*. New York: Wiley.

Sue, D. W., & Sue, D. (1990). *Counseling the culturally different: Theory and practice* (2nd ed.). New York: Wiley.

Witt, J. C., & Elliott, S. N. (1985). Acceptability of classroom management strategies. In T. R. Kratochwill (Ed.), *Advances in school psychology*, (Vol. 4, pp. 251-288). Hillsdale, NJ: Erlbaum.

Zins, J. E., Curtis, M. J., Graden, J., & Ponti, C. R. (1988). *Helping students succeed in the regular classroom: A guide for developing intervention assistance programs.* San Francisco: Jossey-Bass.

Zins, J. E., & Ponti, C. R. (1990). Best practices in school-based consultation. In A. Thomas & J. Grimes (Eds.), *Best practices in school psychology-II* (pp. 673-69). Washington, DC: National Association of School Psychologists.

School-Based Support Groups for Children of Divorce

Neil Kalter
Shelly Schreier
University of Michigan

SUMMARY. Parental divorce touches the lives of approximately one-third of children growing up in the United States. Although many youngsters are able to negotiate the life changes set in motion by their parents' divorce, accumulating clinical and research evidence indicates that a substantial minority of children suffer negative sequelae even years after their parents have separated. Children bring these divorce-related problems to school with them. These difficulties include interferences in concentrating on and completing academic tasks, problems in managing anger and conflict with school authorities and peers, disruptive classroom behavior, regressive behaviors and sadness. A time-limited support group intervention is presented. This model is based on the notion that children of divorce frequently encounter specific divorce-engendered stresses as the divorce process unfolds over time. Group sessions focus on these commonly occurring stressors, normalize children's reactions to them, acknowledge and articulate painful feelings and conflicts, and offer coping strategies to deal more effectively with them. Youngsters readily and enthusiastically participate in these groups. Research indicates that this intervention can be helpful in the short- and long-run.

Address correspondence to: Dr. Neil Kalter, 527 East Liberty Street, Suite 203, Ann Arbor, MI 48104.

[Haworth co-indexing entry note]: "School-Based Support Groups for Children of Divorce." Kalter, Neil, and Shelly Schreier. Co-published simultaneously in *Special Services in the Schools* (The Haworth Press, Inc.) Vol. 8, No. 1, 1993, pp. 39-66; and: *Promoting Student Success Through Group Interventions* (ed: Joseph E. Zins, and Maurice J. Elias) The Haworth Press, Inc., 1993, pp. 39-66. Multiple copies of this article/chapter may be purchased from The Haworth Document Delivery Center [1-800-3-HAWORTH; 9:00 a.m. - 5:00 p.m. (EST)].

The dramatic rise in the number of children experiencing parental divorce in the United States between 1960 and 1980 is well documented. In the years immediately preceding 1960 approximately 10% of minor children saw their parents divorce; by the late 1970s this figure nearly tripled, approaching 30% (Furstenberg, Nord, Peterson, & Zill, 1903; Glick, 1979). Projections based on these national data suggest that over one-third of all children growing up in the United States in the 1990s will experience at least one parental divorce. Though there has been a slight decline in the divorce rate during the 1980s, over one million children per year between 1973 and 1987 have had their family life disrupted by divorce (National Center for Health Statistics, 1990).

The increasingly visible phenomenon of marital disruption has spawned an exploding body of literature aimed at investigating the potential effects of parental divorce on the developmental trajectory of the children involved. One clear consensus has been established: parental divorce results in pronounced negative short-term effects on the academic performance, social adjustment and emotional well-being of the children involved (e.g., Guidubaldi & Perry, 1984; Hetherington, Cox, & Cox 1979; Wallerstein & Kelly, 1980). These studies show that children of divorce are more likely than their counterparts from intact families to have problems in academic performance, the management of anger and aggression, the development of a solid sense of self-worth, and the establishment of mutually satisfying peer relationships.

Within the school setting, these difficulties can surface in a variety of forms. Some youngsters suffer comparatively silently, evidencing sadness, isolation from peer relationships, and regressive behaviors. Others are more disruptive, expressing their divorce-related reactions in a combative or provocative posture vis-a-vis school authorities and conflicts with peers. In each of these scenarios the ability of youngsters to concentrate on, complete and perform well on academic tasks can be compromised as their private divorce agenda takes precedence over the learning process.

That divorce affects the majority of youngsters so profoundly in the short-run is more than sufficient reason to be concerned about this phenomenon. However, an even more disturbing consensus appears to be emerging: namely, that a substantial number of children appear to be burdened by long-term divorce related sequelae. Although there were early hints of this possibility (e.g., Hetherington, 1972; Kalter, 1977; Kalter & Rembar, 1981; Kulka & Weingarten, 1979; Wallerstein & Kelly, 1980), it was not until the mid-1980s that clinical and research evidence began to accumulate regarding the painful legacy of parental divorce carried by many youngsters (e.g., Guidubaldi & Perry, 1985; Hetherington, Cox and Cox, 1985; Kalter, Riemer, Brickman, & Chen, 1985; Wallerstein, 1985, 1987). These conceptually and methodologically diverse studies, conducted completely independently of one another, indicated that many children of divorce continue or begin to experience disruptions to their development years after their parents divorce. In school, problems in academic performance, peer relationships, and conflict with authorities continue.

To better understand both short- and long-term sequelae of parental divorce, Kalter (1987, 1990) has proposed that divorce be viewed as a process extended in time rather than as a circumscribed trauma or crisis. This process conception of divorce, and children's reactions to it, suggests that parental divorce sets in motion a host of significant life changes for the family, and that each such change can constitute a significant stressor in the lives of children. The continuation of stressful life circumstances, initially present at the time of parental divorce, coupled with the unfolding of new stresses as the divorce process proceeds, helps us understand better the basis for long-term divorce related sequelae for so many children. Further, such a perspective leads naturally to the development of specific foci when planning interventions aimed at forestalling or ameliorating the effects of parental divorce for children. If we understand what it is about parental divorce that causes youngsters so much distress over an extended period of time, we are in a better position to construct interventions that will be helpful to them.

Divorce can be seen as potentially creating several powerful stresses for children. First among these is *interparental hostility.* Though not all divorces are suffused with the rage and hurt of one or both parents, many are indeed characterized by such intense feelings. Further, those who work with divorcing families are impressed by how frequently hostilities between parents persist for years after "the divorce." Children bring their reactions to their parents' warfare to school. Some become provocative with school authorities and/or peers as they replay hostilities learned at home.

A second significant stressor for many youngsters is *the loss of or substantial reduction in an ongoing relationship with one parent*, typically the non-resident father. In a nationally representative study, Furstenberg and Nord (1985) found that 23% of fathers had no contact at all with their children in the five years preceding the study and another 20% had not seen their youngsters during the immediately preceding year. The sense of painful loss, rage and self-blame that these children often experience can result in substantial interference in academic progress and the development of appropriate satisfying peer relationships.

A third important source of stress for children of divorce is *parental dating and remarriage*. The vast majority of divorced parents date and most remarry (Furstenberg et al., 1983). These changes can stimulate anger, sadness, anxiety, loyalty conflicts, and sexual curiosities and excitement in many children (Kalter, 1990). In school, youngsters whose parents are dating or have recently remarried evidence, at times, a preoccupation with sexual feelings and ideas, anger, and/or sadness. Collectively, these three sources of ongoing and/or newly emerging sources of stress for youngsters across the extended divorce process indicate key issues that children of divorce frequently must confront and cope with in order to continue a positive, adaptive developmental trajectory.

RATIONALE AND AIMS FOR SCHOOL-BASED DIVORCE SUPPORT GROUPS

To address the significant public health problems noted in the foregoing review, affecting so many of our nation's citizens, the Family Styles Project at the University of Michigan began in 1981 to develop a time-limited, group intervention aimed at facilitating the social-emotional growth of elementary school age children whose parents had separated or divorced. This *developmental facilitation* model is intended to help youngsters confront and adaptively cope with difficult feelings and problematic family circumstances which are so often part of the complex and ongoing divorce mosaic. By doing so, interferences in academic progress can be reduced. We have developed two modules to this intervention; one for children in grades one through three (The Early Elementary School module) and one for youngsters in grades four through six (The Later Elementary School module). A third intervention targeted to seventh through ninth graders (The Junior High School module) is in its final stages of completion and will be available in 1993. This article focuses on the elementary school modules which have enjoyed widespread use, have been evaluated systematically, and have detailed leaders' implementation manuals (Kalter & Associates, 1985, 1988).

In order to achieve the general aim of preventing or reducing the social-emotional and academic problems associated with parental divorce for children, our intervention has *four specific goals*. First, we seek to *normalize* children's status as coming from a family in which divorce has occurred. While learning that many of their classmates also come from divorced families is helpful, it is not sufficient to reduce feelings of stigma and isolation borne by so many children of divorce. Rather it is the process of sharing private feelings, questions and worries about divorce with other youngsters that permits children to come to understand that their inner concerns are neither bad nor wrong, but are widely experienced among children.

Second, we try to *clarify* divorce related issues that may be upsetting or confusing to children. Young children often are confused about why and how divorce occurs, while older elementary school children frequently develop inaccurate, privately held views about divorce. For example, beliefs that children's misbehavior causes divorce and that children's unloveability is the reason noncustodial parents visit infrequently or not at all are terribly burdensome to youngsters. Such beliefs can lead to low self-esteem, depression, and anxiety.

Third, we attempt to provide a safe place where children can *experience and understand* emotionally painful aspects of parental divorce. Children naturally avoid powerful, unpleasant feelings such as anger, sadness, fear, and guilt, especially when these feelings arise in the context of parent-child relationships. However, to the extent that such emotional reactions are avoided and swept beneath a carpet within one's mind, a child is likely to evidence externalizing problems as such conflicts are "acted out," and/or internalizing problems to the extent that they are firmly defended against.

Fourth, we seek to promote the *development of coping skills* to manage troublesome feelings and family interactions common to parental divorce. Children are then empowered to actively cope with the internal and interpersonal conflicts frequently stimulated by parental divorce.

FORMAT OF THE INTERVENTION

We decided on a *group intervention* for several reasons. First, groups create an opportunity for peer support which we find invaluable in helping children confront and cope with divorce related stresses. Within groups children not only see that other youngsters have experienced parental divorce, but perhaps even more importantly, they come to understand through sharing in the group that they are not alone in having sad, angry, and conflicted feelings about divorce. Second, through a sense of safety afforded by numbers, many children can raise concerns more quickly and fully than when seen individually for counseling. Third, it is more efficient and economical to provide services to groups of youngsters than to individual children. The considerable pressure on resources within school systems makes group interventions attractive on practical grounds given the great number of students affected by divorce.

We elected to develop a *time-limited* intervention. While a more extensive program may prove to be of greater value for children, it would be less likely welcomed within a system which has so much to do on behalf of youngsters. Further, it is possible that many parents would be unwilling to consent to have their youngsters participate in an intervention which seemed too intensive and which removed them from ongoing school activities for an extended period of time.

We settled on a ten to fourteen week model for children in grades one through three and an eight to twelve week intervention for youngsters in grades four through six. The basic model consists of ten and eight sessions, respectively, and can be expanded an additional four sessions each. The Early Elementary School module takes slightly longer to implement than the Later Elementary

School one primarily because there is greater cognitive uncertainty among young children about what divorce means. As such, more time is spent on the meaning of divorce and the material flows at a somewhat slower pace. Groups meet weekly for between 45 and 60 minutes. Typically, groups are conducted during school hours. However, if after school day care is provided on-site, groups can be held then.

The *composition of the groups* is mixed with respect to time since divorce, current living arrangements, grade, and gender. Although some interventions restrict divorce support groups to youngsters whose parents have fairly recently separated (e.g., Stolberg & Garrison, 1985), we find it useful to include children from all stages of the extended divorce process. Students whose parents recently have separated can see from group interactions with "veterans" of divorce that there is indeed life after divorce. Children whose parents separated years ago can return to earlier, perhaps buried, reactions they may have had to their parents' divorce as they observe other youngsters wrestle with their immediate reactions to divorce. In addition, including children from various points along the temporarally extended divorce continuum permits a fuller treatment of issues such as residential moves, parent dating and remarriage which unfold over time.

Diversity in the group with respect to current living arrangements has similar advantages to including children from different phases of the divorce process. Children who live in a single parent home with mother learn from their peers who live with their single parent father. And youngsters in these single parent living arrangements offer and receive a different perspective from those who have acquired step-parents (and perhaps step- and/or half-siblings).

Within each module, some variation with respect to grade may be represented in a particular group. However, children are never, by definition of the modules (i.e., Early vs. Later Elementary School), more than two grades apart. The cognitive and social-emotional developmental differences across grade levels is considerable in the elementary school years. Although some cross-grade representation can be useful, as it is in education generally, we have found that it is important to restrict differences along the grade dimension in order to make the group experience meaningful and understandable to all members and to facilitate a sense of group cohesion.

We find it useful to include both boys and girls in our groups. Not only does this accurately reflect the broader school environment, but again, it affords group members a more diverse sense of the divorce experience. Having same-sex groups can facilitate group cohesion (we have conducted them), but at the expense of the aforementioned opportunities in mixed gender groups.

We suggest having between four and seven youngsters in a group. Fewer than four members leads to some sessions in which only two or three children are present due to school absences. This reduces the important sense of safety in numbers which can then interfere with comfortable expression of ideas and feelings. On the other hand, more than seven group members reduces the "air time" for individual children. Groups begin to take on a lecture quality in which youngsters passively receive information instead of actively expressing and processing their experiences.

We initially chose a *co-leader model,* preferably with female-male pairs, because the nature of our role-playing methods, especially in the Later Elementary School module, is facilitated by having such a co-leader format. However, as we gained more experience with our model, we observed other additional reasons for this arrangement. First, having two leaders facilitates the work of the group. Expectable management issues surface as children will occasionally giggle, interrupt one another, become restless, whisper, and tease as emotion-laden topics are raised. The presence of two group leaders permits them to take turns; one attending to the individual management issues while the other continues with the rest of the group. Second, as children observe the co-leaders working together it implicitly models a cooperative, mutually respectful relationship between a man and a woman. Many children of divorce have never directly experienced this phenomenon. Third, since there are boys and girls in a group, all members will have a same-sexed leader available as a role model as well as for the special understanding that some children feel comes from an adult of the same gender as theirs.

As others began to use our model, it quickly became apparent that many schools are not able to provide a male and female co-leader. Some schools do not have the economic resources to have two leaders per group, while in other settings, especially small elementary schools there is not an available male school professional in the building. We have worked with special services providers and staff in several school systems to adapt our co-leader model for use with a single leader. Because our Early Elementary module made extensive use of puppets, we began by having one group leader conduct the puppet play. This went so smoothly that we then suggested that puppets, rather than role play, be used in the Later Elementary module as well. School professionals across a variety of settings report that this appears to work well. In fact some staff prefer solo group leading to co-leading because the need to coordinate style and approach with another leader is not necessary.

It is important to note here what the *leader qualifications* are for conducting these groups. We have had special services providers, classroom teachers, principals, graduate and undergraduate college students and volunteer adults co-lead (or lead on their own) our intervention. This model does not require specialized education or training. Rather, it is important for leaders to have a first-hand sense of what children are like, enjoy being with children, appreciate the stresses divorce can cause for youngsters, and understand the indirect ways in which elementary school students often express the conflicts that they experience. The overwhelming majority of group leaders have told us that the implementation manuals (Kalter and Associates, 1985, 1988) are sufficiently detailed, clear, and filled with examples that they quickly feel a sense of mastery in conducting these groups.

Finally, we have conducted our groups in a wide variety of school settings. They have been located in urban, suburban and rural areas. The full spectrum of family socioeconomic circumstances has been represented, from economically and educationally disadvantaged populations to the very well-educated and well-to-do. Further, our groups have been conducted in schools whose students are predominantly white, African-American, Hispanic, and French-Canadian. Because this intervention can be tailored to specific issues arising within a particular group, leaders have been able to ensure that themes salient to the children are represented. For example, among more economically disadvantaged populations, children report (accurately) that there often is considerable threat of physical violence between their parents and toward them. This *reality* is acknowledged and coping strategies such as calling a nearby relative, leaving the house briefly, and calling the emergency telephone number (9-1-1) are stressed. By contrast, children from middle- and upper-middle class families frequently report frightening *fantasies* of violence between angry parents. This is addressed by helping youngsters separate reality from their fantasies and encouraging them to seek support and clarification from each parent with regards to just how safe everyone will be.

While we have found phenotypic differences in how parental divorce is experienced, the basic underlying issues seem remarkably similar across socioeconomic, racial and ethnic groups. What is most important is that group leaders have a clear understanding of families in their community. For example, the adaptive reliance on the extended family among many urban African-Americans needs to be acknowledged both as a source of strength as well as conflict. It provides for more family caregivers which can be reassuring to children amidst divorce, but it also can create powerful intergenerational conflicts between the youngster's parents and grandparents.

CONCEPTUAL BASES FOR DEVELOPMENTAL FACILITATION GROUPS

In a time-limited intervention, it is crucial that important issues are assured coverage. The luxury afforded by open-ended interventions to wait patiently for important matters to arise and unfold gradually simply is not available in short-term work. Instead, structure must be imposed.

We create structure in our groups by addressing *specific themes* that the clinical and research literature indicates are both common and important across the divorce process. Further, we order these themes according to the *temporal sequence* that many children experience as the divorce process proceeds. For example, the theme of pre-divorce parental arguments appears early, followed by the parents' decision to divorce and to tell the children about it. Custody and visitation issues appear next, while parent dating and remarriage come later in the sequence of sessions. We have found that the unfolding of key divorce themes in this naturally occurring order results in a pronounced sense of coherence for the intervention as a whole.

The conceptual heart of this intervention is the twin use of *displacement activities* and *universalizing statements*. Displacement activities are used to present pivotal divorce themes initially within the safety of a "one step removed" format. Displacement methods are well-known to many child therapists. Puppet play, drawing, story telling, and the use of doll or action figures are used in traditional, individual play therapy. These activities permit youngsters to begin to become more aware of and confront their thoughts and feelings about potentially upsetting and conflictual issues. Directly addressing private and conflict-laden concerns (e.g., "How did you feel when your parents told you they were going to get a divorce?") typically is met with uncomfortable silence, an averted gaze, forced noncommittal shrugging, and/or parroting of the adult party line. In contrast, initially presenting such issues in the safety of the middle-distance afforded by displacement techniques, such as discussing an imaginary character in a story (e.g., "How do you think Mary felt when her parents told her they were getting a divorce?"), permits the youngster to begin to have ideas and feelings about his or her own life circumstances. As group members discuss an imaginary child's reactions to parental divorce, they are actively sharing their own concerns. This implicitly becomes clear to children surprisingly quickly, and they then begin spontaneously to discuss their own family's interactions as well as their inner experiences of them.

Universalizing statements are the primary vehicles for group leaders to communicate important information to the group in a manner which makes it possible for children to hear and make use of this knowledge. Universalizing statements also simultaneously serve to normalize children's experiences, questions, and concerns. As is the case for displacement activities, universalizing statements are indirect. For example, if a child suggests that a story figure is frightened by her parents' arguments, and spontaneously goes on to describe a particularly intense verbal battle that occurred between her own parents, a group leader might say, "Most kids, even pretty grown-up kids, get very worried and scared when their parents fight." Note that this universalizing statement is responsive to the group member's inner experience of her parents' hostilities, but without directly addressing that specific girl or the particulars of the parental argument. This technique accomplishes several desirable goals simultaneously: the group member is not put on the spot, so that further participation is not inadvertently discouraged; the feelings expressed are accepted as being widely shared and thus normal (i.e., "most kids" have such reactions); and, the other group members' attention is engaged because the leader's comment is not narrowly directed to one particular child. The use of displacement activities to present crucial themes initially and universalizing statements to impart constructive perspectives and information to group members together permit children to examine, experience, express, and discuss their thoughts, feelings, questions, and concerns about divorce and its aftermath.

INITIATING GROUPS IN THE SCHOOL

There are several steps which are helpful in successfully initiating divorce support groups in schools. First, it is useful to gather information, usually in the form of published materials, such as articles from professional journals and well-respected print media, to present to staff regarding the impact of divorce on children, especially with respect to academic and behavioral problems in school. Second, it is helpful to determine what percentage of a school's student population come from families in which a divorce has occurred. Such data usually can be obtained from routinely collected school records. Though divorce is common, there are some schools that will have a very low percentage of children of divorce (thus making the argument for a group program unconvincing), while many schools will have compellingly high numbers of such youngsters represented in their population. Third, it is important to stress for staff the availability of structured, time-limited group programs and to present information regarding their potential effectiveness.

Finally, it is crucial to have discussions of these issues with school staff (i.e., the instructional and support staff, administrators) because implementing a program of this sort successfully will depend upon the informed cooperation of all school personnel.

It has been our experience that the approaches described above are nearly always successful in garnering enthusiastic support from the majority of school personnel. Once this has been accomplished, it is wise to begin to inform the school's parent community about plans to institute support groups for children whose parents have separated or divorced. Depending upon the particular community, some questions parents have are: Why should the school provide such a service? Will all children be educated about divorce and does this constitute values training? How can such programs help children? Will I have an option about whether or not my child will participate in a divorce support group? Will our child have a choice about being in a group? What specifically will be discussed in these groups? Will my family's privacy be invaded by these group discussions; and so forth.

We have found it enormously useful to hold evening meetings for the entire parent community in which school personnel and group leaders discuss openly the reasons for starting support groups for children of divorce and how they might be implemented. Being prepared to respond to the sorts of questions noted above is especially helpful. It is also useful to communicate about these issues in the parent or school newsletter.

In these communications to parents, we discuss the realistic needs of children to air concerns about divorce. It is helpful, too, to adopt the posture that participation in such groups is strictly voluntary on the part of parents and children and that children can cease group participation at any time. Further, it is important to emphasize (with our approach) that group leaders do not probe or ask children personal questions, but rather present divorce issues in the context of puppet play, stories about imaginary families, and the like. Though we tell parents that children do tend to discuss their personal experiences with their family, they do so only spontaneously and when they feel sufficiently comfortable in the group. These explanations and assurances usually result in the parent community generally being supportive of divorce groups in the schools, and also encourage parents who have experienced a divorce to enroll their children in such groups.

Once a support group program has been initiated, the next step is to *recruit members* for the groups. There are many ways to do this, and we have attempted most of them. Referrals can be solicited from the instructional staff and from special services providers. Group leaders can appear in classrooms, discuss the groups, and ask for youngsters to volunteer for them. Group leaders may call the parents of children who are known, from school records, to have experienced parental divorce and invite them to enroll their children in the program. These methods each have their own difficulties. Recruitment solely by referral frequently results in groups largely composed of behaviorally disturbed youngsters who happen to have a divorce in their family background. The fact that most schools have insufficient resources to serve all or even most youngsters with special needs, makes a support group intervention an attractive program to which seriously troubled and troublesome children can be sent. For many such youngsters divorce related concerns and conflicts are only a background, contributing component to major problems in general adjustment. Brief support groups are not the answer to the needs of these students. However, asking children directly to volunteer for divorce support groups, or personally inviting parents to volunteer their children for these groups, often makes both children and parents unnecessarily uncomfortable and reduces the likelihood of the youngsters joining a divorce support group. Parents who are personally contacted often feel, however incorrectly, that they are being called because the school has observed their children having special problems.

We have chosen a general mailing strategy to invite participation in our divorce support groups, though we will solicit and accept some referrals from school staff. For example, if we plan to conduct our Early Elementary School module, then a mailing is sent to parents of all youngsters in a particular school who are in grades one through three. Such a mailing consists of: a cover letter from the principal introducing the groups and group leaders to the parents; a detailed description of the nature of the groups and how they can be helpful; and, a consent form for parents to return to the school. (Examples of these materials are in both of our group leader implementation manuals.) No special screening of potential group members takes place; all whose parents sign up for them and who agree to participate are accepted.

Generally we find that between 30% and 50% of all children who have experienced a parental divorce are given parental permission to participate in a divorce group. This figure is somewhat higher than Stolberg and Garrison (1985) report for their recruitment-by-referral divorce support groups. Usually, the higher the socioeconomic status of the school community, the higher the consent rate is for participation. In a study of parents who have been divorced but do not consent to have their children participate in a group, it was found that the nonparticipating youngsters are no better (or less) adjusted than those whose parents consent to the intervention, and that non-consenting parents' primary concerns are not wanting to stir up problems in their children and being leery about their family's privacy being invaded (Falk, 1987).

OVERVIEW OF DEVELOPMENTAL FACILITATION GROUP SESSIONS

The Early Elementary School Module

The first session of this intervention is intended to introduce the group leaders and the children to each other and the children to one another, clarify the purpose of the group, establish rules, have the children begin to get comfortable voicing divorce-related issues in each others' presence, and initiate the development of group cohesion.

We begin by having the children and leaders seated in a circle. *Group leaders introduce themselves* and ask the children if they have heard about the group and why we are having it. Usually at least one child mentions that "It's about divorce," or "Divorce stuff." Group leaders can then ask children what divorce is, what it means. Children in grades one through three frequently will be silent at this point, though sometimes a youngster will say "When your parents split up." Group leaders then clarify that, "Divorce means that your parents don't live together any more." Leaders can go on to note that, "Kids often have a lot of questions, feelings and even worries when their parents get a divorce, and even though it's hard at first to talk about this stuff, we've talked to lots of kids, and we know that it helps to talk about it." This serves to clarify the reason for the group.

It is also important that leaders state clearly what the *structure of the groups* will be: they meet for 50 minutes each week (preferably on the same day and in the same quiet, private room) and that there will be ten meetings all together. It is wise to repeat, at the beginning of each session, which number session it is and how many more are left so that children have a firm sense of the flow of the group and its expected ending.

At this point children are asked to *introduce themselves* by saying their name, with whom they live, and when their parents were divorced. To further a sense of group cohesion, members are also asked to say the name of the child who went just before them. After these introductions, children are asked to name as many of the other youngsters as they can remember This latter activity is repeated near the beginning of each of the subsequent sessions. Usually, by the third session, group members have learned each other's names.

Leaders then note that for a group to go well and for everyone to feel comfortable it needs some *rules*. Four rules are introduced by the leaders: (1) anyone may "pass" at any time so they do not have to talk; (2) group members are expected to take turns rather than interrupting each other; (3) teasing (or "putdowns") are not allowed; and, (4) what is said in the group is confidential. The latter usually requires additional explanations such as "what we say is just between us," or "stuff we talk about is top secret." However, leaders give permission for children to tell their parents anything that the group leaders say or do, and anything that the child (him or herself) has said. What other children say or do is confidential. We need to add this elaboration to permit and facilitate child-parent communications.

With 25 minutes or so usually remaining in the session, the leaders introduce the idea of a *group picture*. Children are told that the group is going to make-up an imaginary family. Group leaders then tape to a wall a prepared line drawing of a house on newsprint on posterboard. Group leaders say, "This is the house of a family *before a divorce*." The group is asked to decide on a name for the family. (Last names of group participants are to be avoided for obvious reasons.) The leaders then ask, "Who lives here?" Children nearly always mention a mother, father, brother, sister, baby, and various assorted pets. Then the group leaders tape to the wall another prepared line drawing, this time with two houses represented. The group is informed that this is the *after divorce* picture of the same family they just drew, and ask who lives in each house. Typically, children place mother, girls, babies, and cats in one house and father, boys and dogs in the other. Group leaders make comments such as "Families sure get divided up when divorce happens," "It looks like kids think girls and babies should go with mom and boys should be with their dad," and other such comments which reflect the group's portrayal of the family. Often, however, children raise specific questions or reveal ideas and feelings about divorce. Group leaders answer questions, accept and clarify ideas, and empathize with feelings.

At the very end of the first session, children are given a large piece of paper with a line drawn vertically down the middle. They are asked to make their own "before and after divorce" picture. This permits children to tailor divorce changes to their own situations and affords leaders the opportunity to circulate among the group members and interact quietly with each child individually. This helps the children settle down. Each session (except session two) ends with a personalized drawing exercise (e.g., the before and after divorce picture, what you can do when your parents argue, what you did the last time you visited with the parent you do not live with). Leaders also use the drawing tasks as a way to encourage active *coping* strategies appropriate for this age group.

These drawings also help create a sense of continuity across sessions for young children. To further a feeling of continuity, children either finish drawings begun at the end of the previous session and/or briefly share their completed drawings (for those who wish to) with the group at the beginning of subsequent sessions. Children also take their completed folder or drawings home with them as a reminder of the group.

In session two children construct a group story about a family "headed for divorce." The children, seated in a circle, take turns adding a line to the story (or passing if they prefer) while one of the leaders writes the story on a large piece of newsprint taped to a wall. After several go-rounds, the group is asked to end the story. Each child gives his/her own endings. If there is time remaining, the group leaders comment on various elements of the story (e.g., "It seems like a lot of kids worry about who will take care of them after divorce," "There seems to be a lot of worry about angry feelings getting loose when parents are divorcing"). The group story also serves as a bridge to the next session: session three begins with group leaders going over the story line by line and making universalized statements about the content of the story.

The group before-and-after divorce drawing and the group story are safe displacement activities for children to begin to voice their private thoughts and feelings about divorce. Common themes which emerge in the context of these displacements include fears that neither parent will continue to take care of the children, sadness over not seeing a parent much if at all after the divorce, angry feelings getting out of control, and a powerful wish for parents to reconcile. These young elementary school children seem anxious about having their needs met, worried about anger, sad about separations and continue to express an abiding wish for their parents to reunite.

In sessions three through nine, the primary displacement activity is puppet play. Children take easily to puppets. But puppets are used, rather than the role playing methods of the Later Elementary School module, for another important reason: Puppet play allows young children to differentiate more clearly what is imaginary versus what is real. When role play was attempted with first through third graders, they became unduly anxious because they could not firmly separate the role of group leaders as they enacted angrily arguing parents, caring parents or dating parents from the reality of leaders being adults who are attempting to help children cope with parental divorce. In sessions three through eight, puppet play is used to initiate group discussion and the expression of ideas and feelings about interparental hostility, children learning about the parents' decision to separate, visitation issues, parent dating, and remarriage (including relationships with the stepparent, stepsiblings and half-siblings) in that order. Thus, the chronological sequence of common divorce-related experiences is reflected as the intervention proceeds.

In session nine, the group leaders and children conduct interviews with each other, using puppets, about various facets of divorce. Themes covered up to this point are addressed. Between sessions nine and ten, group leaders construct a divorce newsletter which includes a reproduction of a Polaroid picture of the entire group taken at the end of session nine. (Examples are given in the leaders' manual.) The tenth and final session is devoted to a group-ending party. Children and group leaders have pizza and soft drinks, the newsletter is read aloud, good-bye feelings are discussed, and group members are given their folder of drawings and three copies of the newsletter to take home. The newsletter serves as a concrete remembrance of the group, a gift from the entire group to each child, and a potential vehicle for communicating important divorce issues to parents.

The Later Elementary School Module

The first session of this module begins much as the one for early elementary school youngsters: Children and leaders are seated in a circle, leaders introduce themselves and clarify the purpose of the group, and children introduce themselves. Because the children here are older (in fourth through sixth grade), when they tell the group their name, with whom they live and when their parents divorced, each child says the name of all the group members who have gone before him/her rather than just the name of the immediately preceding child. Children enjoy this "name game," and quickly master the identities of their co-participants and the leaders. The four rules are also introduced by the leaders in this session, much as they were in the Early Elementary School module. Group members quickly grasp the meaning and intent of the rules, including the confidentiality rule.

Our model for later elementary school children uses role-play or skits to present themes and issues. However if only one person is leading the group, puppet play can be substituted for co-leader role playing. Group story telling and the group newspaper are included in this module as additional displacement activities as they were in the Early Elementary School unit.

After making introductions, clarifying the purpose of the group, and establishing rules, the leaders raise the idea of a group story. This proceeds exactly as it does in the groups for younger elementary school children. After several go-rounds, group members are asked to give their own, individual endings to the story. The leaders then go over the story line by line using universalizing statements to normalize the issues raised in the story and as a basis for group discussion. For example, key themes in the group story are anger getting out of control, and children feeling abandoned and unprotected by their parents. Leaders make universalizing comments such as, "It seems that most kids have some pretty big worries about angry feelings getting out of hand and hurting people in their family." This normalizing and empathic comment also serves to stimulate personal statements from group members such as one child saying, "Yeah, when my mom and dad were yelling and shoving each other, I thought one of them would pull out a gun and start shooting." It is common for later elementary school children to express fantasies of raw aggression among family members. Such ideas are interpreted as well as normalized, and expressions of empathy are made. For example, a leader might say, "Maybe what we're talking about is that kids are worried about everyone's angry feelings, even their own, getting out of control when parents argue and get a divorce." This typically elicits further elaborations of anger-based anxiety. The group comes to see that management of angry feelings is an important issue for children of divorce.

Note that unlike the first session for children in early elementary school grades, we do not use the before-and-after divorce drawings. Children in later elementary school grades are far less confused about what divorce means and are more capable of abstract thinking. As such, we do not need to spend as much time in activities which are intended to cognitively clarify in concrete ways the meaning of the term "divorce."

In the second session, leaders begin by reminding the children which session this is and how many meetings remain. Children are invited to play the name game to further a sense of mutual comfort and group cohesion. Then the leaders introduce the idea of a pre-divorce parent argument. Group leaders then begin a skit in which the female leader is preparing dinner. The male leader is returning from work and the group members are the children who are observing their parents. The leaders briefly exchange sarcastic and irritable comments (e.g., "You're late, again," "Are we having that stuff for dinner again?" "Why can't you ever be on time?" "The house is a mess, as usual"). At that point the leaders step out of their roles as bickering parents and ask the group what they think is going on. Typical comments include, "She's mad because he's got liquor on his breath," "He's angry because she's lazy and doesn't care enough to cook a good meal," "She's probably thinking he was having drinks with his secretary," and "He's thinking she just sits around all day talking on the telephone with her friends."

Group leaders listen to children's comments and quickly resume the skit incorporating into the next sequence the ideas offered by the group. This is a significant advantage over using trigger film strips or tapes; the role play can be *tailored* to represent the specific issues raised by a group. After the next segment of role play, the leaders again ask what is happening. Group members elaborate what they think the parental conflict is about and often note that a divorce seems imminent. As was the case for the group story in session one, leaders normalize, empathize with and may interpret the conflicts and concerns that emerge in group discussion. These are cast as universalizing statements such as: "It seems that when parents fight and start talking about divorce, kids try to figure out why it's happening"; "It sounds like kids feel like blaming one or both parents for the fighting, but that's tough because kids love both of their parents" and, "Most kids do have worries about what might happen next if their parents split up." As in groups for early elementary school children, such comments also serve to further group discussion and the expression of ideas and feelings.

Leaders also ask children what they can do when parents argue. This focus on *active coping strategies* is as crucial as surfacing children's feelings and beliefs about various aspects of divorce. Discussing how children can cope sets a tone of potential mastery, and addresses the need to act assertively to reduce pain over divorce conflicts. Suggestions for coping often introduced by children and leaders include going outside to play, going to their room, turning up their radio and calling a grandparent. Such appropriate avoidance strategies are supported by leaders, while wishes to take sides or mediate the parental conflict are normalized but discouraged as being "too big a job for kids."

Sessions three through six use the same sort of stop-action role play to present pivotal divorce issues and to tailor them to the concerns of a particular group's members. Universalizing statements of the type given above permit group leaders to accept, normalize, correct (where desirable), interpret and generally further discussion of the thoughts, feelings and conflicts that emerge from the children. The chronological unfolding of divorce themes parallels that of the Early Elementary School module. The last two sessions, numbers seven and eight in this module, are devoted to interviews aimed at constructing the group newspaper and a group-ending party, respectively, just as in the module for early elementary school youngsters.

Parent Meetings

An important component of this intervention is the opportunity for group leaders and parents to interact with one another. There are two sessions in which parents and leaders come together; one just prior to the children's groups beginning and another shortly after those groups have ended. Each meeting lasts about an hour.

The first parent meeting has two primary purposes: To have leaders introduce themselves and the program to parents, and for parents to share their perspectives and/or concerns about their youngsters with each other and the leaders. First, group leaders introduce themselves to the parents. This is a chance for parents to get a sense of the group leaders. Leaders typically begin by telling the parents who they are, where they are employed, and what experience they have had working with children. Any questions from parents are answered directly and matter-of-factly (e.g., "Where did you go to college?" "How long have you worked with children?" "Are you married?" "Do you have children of your own?"). Next, parents are asked to share some background information about their family such as how long they have been separated or divorced, the names and ages of their children, how they see their children doing, and whether they or their ex-spouse has remarried. This gives group leaders a context within which to place the children in the group. For the Early Elementary School module, this is especially important because young children are so often confused about the timing and occurrence of events.

These mutual introductions usually take 20 minutes or so. In the remaining time, group leaders describe divorce as a process which consists of many different potential changes in the life of a family.

These changes (e.g., open warfare between parents, seeing the non-resident father less frequently or not at all, residential moves, parent dating and remarriage) can be stressful to children and often stimulate questions, feelings and even worries. Leaders emphasize that this is *not* intended to be a group for troubled youngsters, but rather is a way to help *prevent difficulty* by giving children a chance to learn to cope effectively with their divorce-related reactions.

Leaders briefly describe the nature of the groups, focusing on the temporal unfolding of common divorce themes and the use of imaginary figures/families (e.g., puppet play, role play, group story-telling) rather than direct questions to surface children's ideas and feelings and to initiate group discussion about them. The value of group discussions and of the intervention generally is explained in terms of normalizing children's sense of being a child whose parents have divorced, clarifying questions children may have, helping children work through difficult feelings, and teaching group members coping skills. Leaders tell parents of the need for confidentiality in the groups: Leaders will not relay a specific child's concerns to a parent, but children can discuss leaders' comments and their own reactions to parents. Parents are invited to call the leaders at any time during the course of the program if they have questions about the intervention or concerns about their children.

After all of the children's group sessions have been conducted, parents and leaders meet again. The major aims of this meeting are to communicate to parents the nature of the children's concerns and questions, to provide parents with suggestions about how they might cope with these issues, and to elicit feedback from parents about how the children seem to have responded to the group.

Leaders begin by presenting the questions, ideas and feelings that children in that particular group were concerned about. Care is taken to remind parents of the promise of confidentiality, so that statements are cast in such forms as, "Many of the kids in our group had questions about . . . " "Nearly all of the group members had feelings about . . . " and "Just as we found in our other groups, the children in this group had worries about. . . ." A specific example of how this session might begin is given below. "We've enjoyed working with your children. They came up with a lot of issues and we were able to discuss them in constructive ways. We'd like to share the group's questions and concerns with you, but this isn't a formal lecture, so please feel free to say what's on your mind as we proceed. Let's start with a feeling that's very common for kids to have: upset feelings they have when they see their parents arguing or hear one parent put the other one down." Themes are introduced in this manner, and parents often are eager to discuss them.

In this context leaders introduce suggestions for parents to consider about how to help their children cope effectively with divorce-related issues. These include giving children clear permission to love their other parent and enjoy being with him/her without necessarily painting an unrealistically positive picture of that other parent, restricting as best one can ongoing arguments between parents to times when the child is not present, avoiding speaking ill of the other parent within earshot of the child, resisting the temptation to quiz the child about what happens when he/she is with other parent, how to introduce a new dating partner to the child, and so on. We also teach parents how to use displacement activities and universalizing statements to facilitate communication. Parents initially express disbelief about the usefulness of such simple and transparent (to them, at least) methods, but quickly and eagerly take to them as examples are given.

Finally, parents are asked what they have observed about their children over the course of the program, and what suggestions they may have for future groups. Parents are nearly unanimous in noting positive changes, especially reduction in their child's tension, anger and/or sadness and a greater willingness of the child to discuss divorce-related concerns with a parent. Suggestions occasionally in evidence are to have the groups last longer and to conduct the groups each year so that children can repeat this experience. Parents rarely make other suggestions.

VALUE OF SCHOOL-BASED DIVORCE SUPPORT GROUPS

Our Developmental Facilitation model has been used in over 1,500 school sites representing 35 states and two Canadian provinces. We have conducted systematic, quantitative research on this intervention using standardized instruments to measure children's social and emotional adjustment, self-esteem and perception of parents. We have found that immediately after the groups and six months later, children improved significantly in many areas (Kalter,

1986 unpublished manuscript; Garvin, Leber, & Kalter, 1991). Although the patterns of results using several research instruments are complex, overall there is evidence for statistically significant positive changes in children who have participated in our groups.

Informal feedback from parents, teachers, children, and group leaders has been notably positive. Parents and teachers report that over the course of this intervention, group members became less anxious, sad and/or angry and are much more willing than ever before to ask questions and voice concerns about their parents' divorce. Group members say that it was helpful to see that they weren't "alone" and that other children have the same problems they had, that it was good to have a place to get feelings out, and that they felt better able to handle worries and upsets (Kalter, Pickar, & Lesowitz, 1984). Group leaders also frequently observed these changes in children and most report that they find the intervention easy and comfortable to implement.

In the only assessment of long-term value to school-based divorce support groups of which we are aware, Rubin (1990) compared children four years after having participated in our groups to a matched control group of youngsters whose parents had divorced but had not been in a divorce group. He found that there were statistically significant differences favoring the good adjustment of graduates of these groups, when compared to controls, on 15 of 37 standardized measures and a trend toward statistical significance on another 7 variables. Further, children who had never participated in our groups made substantially more use of individual and family counseling services than those who had been in a group (54% vs. 14%), yet the group graduates were significantly better adjusted.

There are two other school-based divorce support group programs which also may be characterized as being rigorously developed and systematically assessed; The Divorce Adjustment Program (Stolberg & Garrison, 1985; Stolberg & Mahler, 1989), and the Children of Divorce Intervention Project (Pedro-Carroll & Cowen, 1985; Pedro-Carroll, Cowen, Hightower & Guare, 1986). These investigators also employed standardized measures of social and emotional adjustment and self-esteem in the context of controlled research designs. Their findings are similar to ours for short-term (i.e., six months or less) efficacy of divorce support groups in the schools. Generally, children who participate in the Divorce Adjustment Project and the Children of Divorce Intervention Program (each of which meet weekly for between 10 and 14 sessions) fare better than their peers who do not come across multiple measures of adjustment.

Informal feedback and systematic research indicate that carefully developed, conceptually guided school-based support groups can be helpful to many children whose parents are separated or divorced. However, since neither the divorce process nor children's development are static phenomena, it would be enormously useful to assess whether serial, brief interventions can add to the long-term efficacy of school-based support groups. We have had numerous youngsters participate in our groups several times over a period of years. Does this enhance the effects beyond what is achieved in the first intervention? Much as rereading a good book imparts new meaning and perspectives as we grow and mature, perhaps several experiences in support groups will provide incremental help for children of divorce at various phases of their adjustment to post-divorce family life. Finally, as a resource integrated within the school environment, the youngsters who participate in these groups may well experience the academic community as an arena which promotes and supports social and emotional well-being as well as cognitive development–to the benefit of all.

REFERENCES

Falk, J. (1987). *Preventive intervention services for children of divorce: An assessment of who uses the program*. Unpublished doctoral dissertation. University of Michigan, Ann Arbor.

Furstenberg, F.F., & Nord, C.W. (1985). Parenting apart. *Journal of Marriage and the Family, 47,* 893-904.

Furstenberg, F.F. Jr., Nord, C. W., Peterson, J.L., & Zill, N. (1983). The life course of children of divorce: Marital disruption and parental contact. *American Sociological Review, 48,* 656-668.

Garvin, V., Leber, D., & Kalter, N. (1991). Children of divorce: Predictors of change following preventive intervention. *American Journal of Orthopsychiatry, 61*(3) 438-447.

Glick, P. (1979). Children of divorce in demographic perspective. *Journal of Social Issues,* 35, 170-182.

Guidubaldi, J., & Perry, J.D. (1984). Divorce, socioeconomic status, and children's cognitive-social competence at school entry. *American Journal of Orthopsychiatry, 54*, 459-468.

Guidubaldi, J., & Perry, J.D. (1985). Divorce and mental health sequelae for children: A two year follow-up of a nation wide sample. *Journal of the American Academy of Child Psychiatry, 24*, 531-537.

Hetherington, E.M. (1972) Effects of father absence on personality development in adolescent daughters. *Developmental Psychology, 7*(3), 313-326.

Hetherington, E.M., Cox, M., & Cox, R., (1979). Play and social interaction in children following divorce. *Journal of Social Issues, 35*, 36-49.

Hetherington, E.M., Cox, M., & Cox, R. (1985). Long-term effects of divorce and remarriage on the adjustment of children. *Journal of the American Academy of Child Psychiatry, 23*, 518-530.

Kalter, N. (1977). Children of divorce in an outpatient psychiatric population. *American Journal of Orthopsychiatry, 47*, 40-51.

Kalter, N. (1987). Long-term effects of divorce on children: A developmental vulnerability model. *American Journal of Orthopsychiatry, 57*, 587-600.

Kalter, N. (1990). *Growing with divorce*. New York: The Free Press.

Kalter and Associates. (1985). *Time-limited developmental facilitation groups for children of divorce in later elementary school: A preventive intervention*. Unpublished leaders' manual. (Available by writing the senior author at: 527 E. Liberty Street, Suite 203, Ann Arbor, MI 48104).

Kalter and Associates. (1988). *Time-limited developmental facilitation group for children of divorce in early elementary school: A preventive intervention*. Unpublished leaders' manual. (Available by writing to the senior author at: 527 E. Liberty Street, Suite 203, Ann Arbor, MI 48104).

Kalter, N., & Rembar, J. (1981). The significance of a child's age at the time of parental divorce. *American Journal of Orthopsychiatry, 51*, 85-100.

Kalter, N., Riemer, B., Brickman, A., & Chen, J.W. (1985). Implications of parental divorce for female development. *Journal of the American Academy of Child Psychiatry, 24*, 538-544.

Kulka, R., & Weingarten, H. (1979). The long-term effects of parental divorce in childhood on adult adjustment. *Journal of Social Issues. 35*, 50-78.

National Center for Health Statistics (1990). Advance report of final divorce statistics, 1987. *Monthly Vital Statistics Report*, 38 (Suppl. 2.) Hyattsville, MD: U.S. Public Health Service.

Pedro-Carroll, J., & Cowen, E.L. (1985). The Children of Divorce Intervention Project: An investigation of the efficacy of a school-based prevention program. *Journal of Consulting and Clinical Psychology, 53*, 603-611.

Pedro-Carroll, J. Cowen, E., Hightower, A., & Guare, J. (1986). Preventive intervention with children of divorce: A replication study. *American Journal of Community Psychology, 14*, 277-290.

Rubin, S. (1990). *School-based groups for children of divorce: A four-year follow-up evaluation*. Unpublished doctoral dissertation, University of Michigan, Ann Arbor, MI.

Stolberg, A., & Garrison, K. (1985). Evaluating a primary prevention program for children of divorce. *American Journal of Community Psychology, 13*, 111-124.

Stolberg, A., & Mahler, J. (1989). Protecting children from the consequences of divorce: An empirically derived approach. *Prevention in Human Services*, 7(1), 161-176.

Wallerstein, J.S. (1985). Children of divorce: Preliminary report of a 10 year follow-up of older children and adolescents. *Journal of the American Academy of Child Psychiatry, 24*, 545-553.

Wallerstein, J.S. (1987). Children of divorce: report of a ten year follow-up of early latency-age children. *American Journal of Orthopsychiatry, 57*, 199-211.

Wallerstein, J., & Kelly, J. (1980). *Surviving the break-up: How children and parents cope with divorce*, New York: Basic Books.

The Invisible Griever: Support Groups for Bereaved Children

Mary Ann Healy-Romanello

Hamilton County (OH) Office of Education

SUMMARY. Many people are equipped, through crisis intervention strategies and plans, to handle the immediate ramifications of a death within a particular school or community system. However, after the crisis has passed the question generally surfaces as to how one can help the children who have been greatly impacted by the death and are in the midst of the grieving process. The grieving child has often been invisible to adult caregivers like counselors, teachers, and school psychologist. The means of helping a child who has experienced a death in his family can be greatly enhanced by the development of grief support groups. Through the use of support groups children can learn to share their feelings, discover that they are not alone, and move through the grieve process.

For the past five years, hundreds of children have come together twice a month to talk about the death of a parent or sibling at Fernside: A Center for Grieving Children, in Cincinnati, Ohio. The support groups were formed in response to parents' recognition that

---

Address correspondence to: Dr. Mary Ann Healy-Romanello, Hamilton County Office of Education, 11083 Hamilton Avenue, Cincinnati, OH 45231-1499.

[Haworth co-indexing entry note]: "The Invisible Griever: Support Groups for Bereaved Children." Healy-Romanello, Mary Ann. Co-published simultaneously in *Special Services in the Schools* (The Haworth Press, Inc.) Vol. 8, No. 1, 1993, pp. 67-89; and: *Promoting Student Success Through Group Interventions* (ed: Joseph E. Zins, and Maurice J. Elias) The Haworth Press, Inc., 1993, pp. 67-89. Multiple copies of this article/chapter may be purchased from The Haworth Document Delivery Center [1-800-3-HAWORTH; 9:00 a.m. - 5:00 p.m. (EST)].

they were not equipped to deal with their children's grief. As one parent stated, "Some days, just getting my own shoes on was all that I could accomplish." Parents felt defenseless as they saw the pain of their children, believing that there was very little that they could do to help them.

This article is an overview of the work performed at Fernside. At the time of Fernside's inception in 1987, there was a scarcity of guidelines in the professional literature that addressed the grieving child or recognized the need for specific support groups for children. Much of what was written was taken from the adults' perspective of the grieving process. The title, "invisible griever," was often used to address the facts that children were often forgotten by society as a whole in the grieving process, and that little was known about the steps in working with groups of grieving children.

Support groups for grieving children within the school structure have long been ignored as a means on intervention. This omission in large part has been due to a reluctance to discuss or even identify death and grieving issues. The fact is that thousands of school age children die each year, and one out of seven children loses a parent to death before the age of 10 (Lord, 1990). This statistic may be surprising when one looks at the lack of attention that has been directed toward the grieving child. However, there has been a tremendous increase in the literature on this topic in the past ten years (Cassini & Rogers, 1985, 1990; Lewis, 1991; Linn, 1982; Morganett, 1990; Rando, 1984; Worden, 1982). The emergence of this literature suggests that the recognition of grieving children, along with means of supporting them, is beginning to be addressed by professionals in school and other settings.

The purposes for support groups which focus on the grieving child are many. Grieving children often do not have a familial or peer support network. The death of a parent or sibling effects the entire family. Since other family members are also grieving, the child's family support system may not function as constructively as it had in the past, or it may be nonexistent. Due to the debilitating effect of a death on the entire family, the child may be in need of support from an outsider.

The grieving child's overt actions are often perceived as indications that he or she is no longer grieving, was too young to understand the concept of death, or did not need to be involved in death issues. The reality, however, is very different. Children do grieve, although their means of grief may be misidentified. Teachers, counselors, school psychologists, and other special services staff are significant others in the child's life who can be especially effective during this time.

Peers may not be supportive of the grieving child. Friends may not know what to say to the child and are often afraid to interact with a child who has had someone die in the family. The grieving child also can be confronted with cruel statements from peers whose fears about death are dealt with by taunting and degrading the child. One fourth grade student with whom we worked was told by his peers that he could no longer play on the baseball team because he didn't have a father who could practice with him. A fourth grade girl was told that she was an orphan because her father had died, and many children have reported being told that they were bad, didn't pray hard enough, or in some way were responsible for the death of their parent or sibling.

Other adults may also become distant from the grieving child for fear of not saying the right thing, and hence do not say anything at all. Many of the children at Fernside have commented on the positive and the negative responses they received from school personnel. Many of the children appreciated the fact that teachers, principals, and counselors attended the funeral or memorial service for their parent or sibling. They also appreciated the help that was given to them upon returning to school. At the same time the children have recalled horror stories of being told to stop crying or that they would get over it in time. In one child's words, "My teacher didn't come, no one from school did. At the funeral I didn't miss them or anything, but then later I got to thinking that no one from the school came. No one said anything to me either." Some of the children from Fernside have also discussed the fact that expectations, especially in regard to academic performance, were not altered. The children were expected to maintain the same grades, participate in class and carry on as if life had not been permanently and significantly changed.

A GROUP APPROACH TO SUPPORTING GRIEVING CHILDREN

When all of a child's support networks, family, friends, peers, and school personnel, are dismantled or barely functioning, it becomes painfully clear that grief groups can serve an extremely important function for the child. The emphasis of such groups is placed on support, not therapy or behavioral changes. Children are in need of a respite where they can take off their masks of the "good grievers" and be themselves. They need support from people who will let them know that the feelings they have are not indications of craziness or maladjustment. They need to be around other children who have also experienced a loss, to know that they are not alone, and they need to hear how other children have learned to cope with their losses.

Before addressing how to establish groups, issues related to the grieving child are discussed. These include a summation of the grief process, what we do know about children's grief, and a profile of what the grieving child looks like.

Children face many of the same issues that adults face when someone dies in the family, including guilt over conflicts with the person who died, inability to openly talk about socially unacceptable deaths such as suicide, or having a death negated due to an event like an extended illness. A primary difference between an adult's grief and a child's grief is that the child's grief is often unseen. Depending on the child's age he or she may lack the experiences, cognitive capabilities, the expressive language, and the autonomy to resolve the loss. Children also may not have the vocabulary needed to label and discuss their feelings, and lack early mastery of loss experiences which they could draw upon in terms of coping with the shock and pain. A network of support may not be functioning as other family members are also grieving and peers do not know how to help. The following explanation of the grief process may be helpful in gaining an understanding of the process used in grief work. The explanation of the process is derived from Burrell (1989), a parent who experienced the death of his son. This description is similar to that found in the published literature (e.g., Jackson, 1971).

The Grief Process

The grief process can be visually displayed as an open circle. The top of the circle represents the death of a family member. At the time of this event a person's reactions can be labeled as shock, numbness, or denial. The person finds it too hard to believe that it is true. The reactions, which occur soon after the death, can include: guilt, anger, resentment, depression, helplessness, pain, relief, and sadness. Guilt feelings stem from the possible belief that the surviving person could have done something to prevent the death, a "What if" or "If only," feeling. Guilt may also arise from feelings of having said the wrong thing or wishing that something else had been said before the person had died. Anger can also be unidirectional. It can be imposed upon the person who died, "Why did you leave me?" or "Why me?" Pain can be both physical and mental and include such factors as fatigue, appetite increase or decrease, insomnia, headaches, and nightmares. Feelings can also be mixed such as relief and guilt. Relief may occur in terms of the person no longer being in pain, but then guilt may arise as a result of feeling that way. These feelings are not unique in and of themselves and continue in one way or another throughout the grief process.

There are no clear cut stages such as sadness for two days, guilt for one, and then acceptance. During the first year feelings are experienced as waves and may ebb and flow. Some days the pain may not be as severe and the person feels like things are getting better. Then there are days when the person can not function at all. These times appear to be the most debilitating for grieving people because they were making progress, and then suddenly feel worse than before. This point is probably one of the most difficult for the helper to understand as well. The hardest time may not be when the death occurs but after the numbness has worn off. Because there is little evidence to confirm that grieving ends, helping people need to be aware of their own tolerance for frustration at seeing a grieving adult or child repeat some earlier behaviors.

Support groups, help offered by friends, teachers, counselors, and school psychologists can be especially beneficial when the person's feelings are fluctuating. This is often a time when initial support from friends, which occurred during the time of the death, has waned. The person may feel more alone, the feelings of pain may reoccur, and thoughts of getting stuck and not being able to resolve the painful feelings become prevalent. There can even be feelings of guilt as the surviving person finds him or herself doing things that they thought they would never be able to do again. Recovery from the loss of a loved one is work that entails laboring through the pain and venting the sorrow. It is frustrating because the cycle swings back and forth from feelings of acceptance of the death to increased pain.

The second year can bring flashbacks and a resumption of personal grief for the survivor. This personal grief entails acknowledgement that the survivor has been changed by the death and by the grief. Finally, at some indeterminate time, the survivor can view the death, the loved one who died, and themselves, not without pain and sadness, but also with future hope, healing and growth. The circle comes full cycle but never closes as grief is an ongoing process.

Grief at Various Ages

Surviving children are more easily lost in the grieving process and depend upon members of the family, teachers, and other important adults for assistance in coping. Many variables factor into the grief process of the child. Sex, age, birth order, family functioning, divorce, cause of the death, cultural considerations, and religious and cultural rituals of death are but a few. Other variables include what the child has been told about the death, what the child has been told to say, whether or not the child holds a parent or himself responsible, and the type of peer support given to the child. The variables which effect the grief process are many as should be our own responses, as each child's story is unique.

Knowledge of possible cognitive and emotional responses to death are necessary in order to gain a sense of the child's perspective. However, it is important to realize that the cognitive and emotional responses are only a few of the variables which will impact upon the child and the grieving process. The following is provided as a general guide rather than as specific delineation of cognitive and emotional responses. Younger children can demonstrate the capabilities attributed to older ages, and at the same time older children may regress to younger forms of behavior.

Infant to age two. Children at this age do not have a concept "perse" of death. However, they can sense that things in the environment are different and can react to emotional changes in the caregiver. If the caregiver is emotionally upset over a death, the young child may react to the emotional changes. Differing behavior can occur in sleep patterns, eating routines, and general disposition.

Three to five. The child at this age does not understand the concept of death. These children believe that death is reversible and that people come back to life. They also believe that the dead body continues to function as if the person were still alive (e.g., eats, breathes, etc.). The response to the death may vary in terms of asking inappropriate questions, being repetitive in questioning, and possibly regressing in some behaviors (bedwetting, clinging, and separation anxiety). This age child often makes faulty connections between facts such as: since grandpa died in the hospital, everyone who goes to the hospital dies. The belief in magical thinking is also prevalent at this age, which can allow children to believe that they were in some way responsible for the death. The major fears of these and younger children are related to separation and security (Who will take care of me?).

Six to twelve. At this age children begin to develop an understanding that death is final, but may still fear that the person will come back to life. They are more apt to ask for detailed explanations of the death, and may need someone to explain and give permission to express the wide range of feelings that they are experiencing. The major fear of these children is the possible deaths of the surviving parent or siblings. The child can become so overwhelmed with this fear that he may lose the capacity to sleep, eat or be out of sight of the surviving family members.

Adolescence. The adolescent is developmentally able to understand the finality of death and the impact that a death may have on the family, even to the point of knowing how it will effect economic security and other aspects of life. The developmental task is to learn how to cope with change, loss, growth, and grief. Death at this time of development is different from the younger ages because adolescents are in the process of becoming totally independent from their parents. There can be unresolved issues which center around personal autonomy and independence from parental care. The adolescent may regress in terms of feeling the need to stay home and take care of the family, an action which may hinder independent growth. On an emotional level, most adolescents attempt to understand the philosophical and religious issues which center around death.

There are a variety of emotional responses which children can display after the death of a loved one. These include but are not limited to: denial, bodily stress, aggression, anxiety, panic, guilt, magical thinking, and taking on characteristics of the deceased person. Everyone grieves differently. Some children grieve by acting out, fighting, biting, or throwing things. Others exhibit behaviors of retreat, defeat, or withdrawal. Still other children appear to show no visible signs of grief; they seem to be as happy and accepting as before the death. The truth is that there are many healthy and unhealthy ways of grieving.

In order to understand how children grieve and thus how adults can help them through the process, we need to gain a sense of the child's perspective, to understand the world from the child's point of view. As a young boy at Fernside said, "Tell them that we understand. Tell them that we know death is sad."

Major Themes in Children's Grief

A number of recurrent grief themes have been documented at the Fernside Center. These themes have been discussed by many of the children, and are used as a means of framing the group sessions. The themes include: (1) all deaths of a loved one are violent and the world is perceived as a dangerous and painful place; (2) a continuing set of fears about the death of other loved ones; (3) a feeling of being lost when the surviving adults are themselves engulfed in the grief process; (4) feeling defeated when teachers ignore or criticize their grief process; (5) going back and forth in their development as grieving people; (6) timeless grief; (7) help can be provided by simple acts of caring and by making the school environment a place for comfort, security, and acceptance; (8) children are capable of "teaching" about their grief if they are encouraged to express their feelings in a safe environment; and (9) children learn to look at the death and themselves with hope and growth.

Every child's story is unique as an experiential happening. Each child perceives their story as a unique one, only happening to them. However, the use of themes allows the children to see that others have experienced similar feelings even if the events are not exactly the same. As one young child reported, "There isn't enough time. No, we don't have enough time for me to tell you what happened. Even if we were here for days or weeks there wouldn't be enough time."

ESTABLISHING GRIEF SUPPORT GROUPS

Much work needs to be accomplished before groups are introduced in schools. Included is work with the family and teaching staff. It is beyond the scope of this article to discuss how to handle talking to the class about the death of a peer's parent or sibling, or how to accommodate a child's reentry into school. However, Cassini and Rogers (1990) have written an excellent reference for parents and teachers which discusses the step-by-step procedures for working with a grieving child.

The greatest problem in establishing grief groups within the school system primarily rests with the adults rather than the children. Before beginning to deal with grieving children, the helper needs to assess many personal points related to grief, as well as assist the classroom teacher's work with a grieving child. The challenge in learning about grief and how to assist the grieving child is an arduous task. On a personal level it entails identification of personal biases and beliefs about grief, and then putting these notions aside so that the words and the world of the child can be understood. The helping adult needs to be cognizant of his or her own biases of "healthy grieving," such as, children should grieve by showing or not showing tears, and/or showing or not showing anger. Imposing a grieving structure usually forces the child to become a "good griever," to wear a mask so that adults in the environment will be appeased. Such a behavior is merely a performance for the parent, the counselor, or the teacher. It forces the child to hide true feelings, attitudes, and the behaviors that the helper may dislike, feel are inappropriate, or believe to be wrong.

With regard to leader preparation, adults must have a working knowledge of the grief process, group process, and a clear understanding of their own views on death and loss issues. Training in both grief and group processes would be extremely valuable. (Recommended readings on grief include: Bowlby, 1969, 1973, 1980; Cassini & Rogers, 1985; Engel, 1980; Grollman, 1976, 1981; Linn, 1982; Rando, 1984; Rofes, 1985; and Worden, 1982.) If possible, groups should be co-facilitated as a means of processing the interactions of the children. It is also necessary for the adults to be able to process their own feelings and thoughts about what the children have said. Hearing stories about grief, especially those of children, can be very painful. Any interested staff member, teacher, adult involved in grief ministry through religious affiliations, community mental health personnel, and counselor or school psychology graduate student could serve as co-facilitators.

It is imperative that consultation take place with the teacher(s) to prepare the class for the child's return to school. The time between the death and the return of the grieving child can be valuable in helping other children understand the grieving process, learn what to say to a grieving child, and even discuss some of their own losses. The goal is to help the other children understand their own feelings, find words to express their feelings to the grieving child, and to make the classroom environment a safe and comfortable place for the returning child. Often, teachers also need this time to talk to someone about their own fears and beliefs related to death issues. Upon the child's return to school procedures can be discussed regarding the provision of a quiet place to go when he or she is feeling sad, the availability of a phone to call home, and identification of specific people who are available for counseling.

Group Structure

The support groups are not counseling or therapy centered groups. There is no step-by-step procedure that, if followed correctly, will eliminate the pain. And, there are no short cuts. The goals are simple in that the support groups are designed to address the emotional needs of the children in an atmosphere of mutual trust, acceptance, and unconditional regard. The children are encouraged to share and claim their feelings. The objective is to give children a chance to find their own best answer to working through the grieving process through a group experience.

Grief support groups can be used with preschool through high school populations within a school setting. The best practice is one of grouping children by age rather than type of loss. Young childrens' needs, because of their cognitive and language skills and their lack of experience with loss issues, are best met when they are with same age peers. Children from 6 to 12 years of age appear to have more need for physical activities such as wrestling, working out with batakas, or hitting bop-em clowns. Teenagers, because of their age and need for autonomy and independence, have some different grief issues which would not be appropriately addressed with a younger age group.

The number of children per group will vary. The group needs to be large enough to generate discussion, yet small enough so that all members have an opportunity to talk about their experiences. When possible large discussion groups can be divided into smaller sections to allow for more individualized attention. In order to best meet the needs of the children, groups should be divided into age ranges. The following division may be helpful in deciding which children would work best together: preschoolers, middle-age (6 to 9-years of age), pre-teen (10 to 13 years of age), and teen. If one school facility does not have a large enough grieving population, then combining several schools or offering the groups through a community agency are means of obtaining a sufficient number of children.

Determining a child's readiness for entrance into a grief group can be difficult to assess. Families at Fernside are not brought into groups immediately as the shock and numbness of the death is still a very real thing. In a similar manner, the school age child may need some time to adjust to family changes, and become acclimated to the school situation before joining a support group. Teachers, counselors, school psychologists, and other school personnel can help make the school environment a comforting place and support the child through the initial phases of the grief process. After the child has returned to school and individual support has been initiated, then the child could be invited to join a grief group. It is helpful to encourage the reluctant children that they only need to give the group a chance. If they do not want to stay in the group after two or three sessions then the leader should discuss the matter with their parent(s) and suggest that the child not be forced to stay in the group. Individual assistance can still be provided by other supportive adults. Children are often reluctant to join a grief group because they fear that people will force them to talk, they will start crying, or they will be ridiculed for their feelings. Trust levels, especially when meeting new adults and peers, are generally extremely low as these children are very vulnerable and unsure of their own feelings.

Pre-Entry Background and Preparation

Before a child enters a group, background information should be obtained from the parent or guardian. An intake questionnaire can be used as a means of gathering important information. Some of the questions would involve identification of other family members, who died in the family, cause and date of death, length of illness, what the child has been told about the death, type of burial, other losses (other deaths, divorce, moves, etc.), current concerns of the family, and any other additional information that would help in working with the child. In talking with the parent, it should be stressed that the group is to provide support rather than counseling or therapy. If possible, a meeting for parents or guardians of the families involved in the support group could be arranged so that they could be apprised of basic grief information, and possibly to establish a network for parents.

The children's groups at Fernside meet twice a month from September through June. New members are added as space permits. The number of group meetings, within the school environment, will be dependent upon the leader's time constraints. Bi-monthly meetings are sufficient; however weekly meetings have proven to be extremely helpful as the child does not have to suppress feelings and thoughts for an extended period of time. When possible the grief group should last throughout the school year. If this procedure is not manageable, then a consecutive ten week program followed by monthly group meetings is recommended. Monthly group meetings during the summer are also advisable in order to continue the support. These meetings are less formal and involve picnics, swimming, or other outside activities.

Continuation of the group throughout the school year is important because the grief process is not accomplished in a step-by-step fashion. The child's feelings will fluctuate from week to week or day to day. A child may appear to be fine for the first couple of months and then begin to cry or become anxious for some unknown reason. The knowledge that there will be someone to talk to on a weekly or monthly basis provides the grieving child with a sense of security. The most stressful times for the grieving child are anniversary dates (birth and death date of the person who died), the child's own birthday, the holiday season (from November through December), and other family celebrations.

Overview of Format

Although the groups are supportive in nature, many counseling procedures and formats are used. The use of videos, books, arts, role playing, imagery, relaxation techniques, discussions, communication strategies, and journal writings can all help the children identify and express their feelings. There are a number of excellent books which discuss the death of a grandparent, parent, or sibling, and associated feelings (e.g., Clifton, 1983; Fassler, 1982; Kremitz, 1981; LeShan, 1976; Prestine, 1987). Within this framework, adults are encouraged to share their experiences and feelings about death as a means of providing a role model for the children and to bring up issues that are often kept secret, such as feelings of guilt and anger toward the person who died.

The format of each session consists of four parts: (a) large group discussion where the activities of the session are introduced and members are given a chance to talk about recent or past concerns; (b) small group activity which can then be brought back to the large group and shared; (c) game activity; and (d) closing activity which includes a summation of the session, introduction of topic for the next session, clean up, and farewells. It is not unusual for the entire session to be spent on the children's opening dialogue. At times a member may introduce a topic of specific interest to the group which needs to be addressed immediately. An example of such a topic is how a child may have been teased by other students at school because someone had died in the family. During these times the leaders must put their agenda aside and respond to the group's needs.

GROUP SESSIONS

The primary focus of the first and second sessions is one of trust building. The concept of trust will be one that is carried out throughout the entire group sessions; however, it is an issue which must be consciously worked into the first session so that members begin to feel that they are in a safe environment where they can take off their masks and share their true feelings and pain.

The program goals are to explore, with the students, the grief process and to help them understand the feelings that they have. The first six sessions deal primarily with specific feelings related to the death experience. The additional sessions focus in on (a) the students' return to school after the death and support networks among peers, (b) the idea that the death is sad but that the students are left with cherished memories, special times, or personal gifts from the person who died, and (c) how the student has changed and may be happier. During the holiday season, several sessions can be geared to identifying ways of handling the holidays, a memorial session recognizing the people who have died, or discussing ways the family remembers the person who died (e.g., putting a special ornament on a Christmas tree, planting a tree at the grave, etc.). Other issues which may be of interest to the students include: the funeral experience, saying goodbye to the person who died, and future fears such as who may die next.

We have found the following outline to be appropriate for groups of children ranging in age from seven to twelve. The same themes can be used for older children; however, the activities may need to be altered.

Session One: Introduction

Goals: To help students become acquainted with each other and to feel comfortable in the group; to identify group ground rules, especially related to confidentiality; to explain the concept of a grief group and the goals; and to help students share information on who died (name, relationship, cause of death, date of death, etc).

Materials: Chalkboard/chalk, journals, markers, pens, stickers.

Procedures: Facilitators introduce themselves to the group and have the students introduce themselves along with their age or grade. Explain the concept of a grief group in that it is a group of people who have experienced the death of a parent, sibling, or significant loved one. Members can talk about the person in their life who died and the feelings they have related to the death. Group rules can be established by having members generate guidelines which would help the group function, such as: one person speaks at a time, listen while others talk, no one has to speak–you can pass, no put downs, and confidentiality. Some time should be spent on the issue of confidentiality, especially in regard to the co-facilitators not talking to parents or teachers regarding the specific issues that were discussed, along with members not repeating what others said within the group.

Group Task: Go around the group and ask students to tell who has died, relationship, cause of death, etc. Some children may be reticent about giving any information beyond the fact that a sibling or a parent died. At that point a facilitator could ask some questions, but it is suggested that the child be given time to become acclimated to the group. Additional questions may be the name of the person who died and who else is in the family. Asking for the date of the death is sometimes too hard for younger students to remember. After all of the members and facilitators have offered information to the group, the facilitator could summarize some of the information in order to help make connections. Examples would be to identify all of the children who have had a father loss, unexpected death, etc.

Introduce the idea of journals to the students. The students can write anything in their journal: thoughts about the person who died, how they were feeling that day, reaction to group activities, etc. The last part of the session can be spent on decorating or identifying the individual journals. The children will be able to take the journals home after the last session. If time allows, let the students play games that require interactions as a means of increasing involvement with each other (e.g., The Ungame, or Pictionary).

Closure: Discuss the fact that it can be scary to come to a new group and meet new people. Reiterate that the group is a safe place. Discuss the fact that group time is for them. Provide space to hang any artwork, pictures, or writings.

Session Two: Exploring Feelings

Goals: To identify personal feelings; enlarge feeling vocabulary; and discuss personal views with group members.

Materials: Posterboard, cards with facial expressions, paper, pens, polaroid camera.

Procedures: During this session and all of the following sessions, time should be taken to check with each member in regard to how he or she is feeling and how the past week has gone. Introduce the theme of feelings by discussing how some feelings are hidden deep inside and want to get out. Sometimes the feelings come out a little at a time, while other times they just explode.

Group Task: Divide the group into two teams. Each teams task is to generate as many feeling words as possible within a given time (e.g., 10 minutes). The teams come back and share their feeling words which are written on a large piece of posterboard that all members can see. After the generation of feeling words, each child is handed a facial expression card and asked to tell a story about when they felt that way (e.g., shocked, angry, happy, etc.). These experiences can be written down in the student's journal with the help of the facilitator. As a final activity, the students could demonstrate a feeling with their entire body which can then be photographed. These pictures can be matted and placed on a posterboard under the heading, "How Do You Feel?"

Closure: Finalize the session by discussing the fact that there are many different feelings, and that feelings are not right or wrong. Children who have had someone die in their family will have a lot of different feelings that can make them confused. Stress that it helps to talk about feelings so that people do not have to keep them inside, and that once people share feelings they often find that others have felt the same way.

Session Three: Feelings of Disbelief

Goals: To increase the child's awareness of feelings related to the grief process; to identify feelings of disbelief around the loved ones death; and to introduce the idea of change in self due to the death.

Materials: Journals, long sheets of paper, pens, and markers.

Procedures: Check with students about how things are going. Introduce topic by telling students how facilitator was affected by the death of a loved one or what other students have said in regard to the death of a family member. Relay the idea that upon hearing about the death, one may have felt a feeling of disbelief, or could not believe that it was true. Ask group members if anyone had experienced a similar feeling when told about the death of their family member. Some children may report that they still do not believe the death has occurred, particularly if they were not involved in the funeral or memorial proceedings. The facilitators can respond by acknowledging the fact that it is very hard to believe that someone has died. Validate where the student is and ask him or her what it feels like. Do not confront the student with the fact that the death has occurred.

Group Task: Write down in journals or tape the students' responses to the question on disbelief. Introduce the topic of change by having students do a time line of when they were born, specific events in their lives, the death of the family member, feeling of disbelief, and where they are now (feelings and other changes). Have students talk about their time lines.

Closure: Hang time lines on a wall. Discuss with students the idea that when something sad happens it is very hard to comprehend or believe. Talking about those feelings and asking questions can be helpful.

Session Four: Identifying Feelings of Anger and Guilt

Goal: To identify personal feelings, reactions, or attitudes about the death of a family member; and to identify common feelings of anger and guilt.

Materials: Slips of paper with incomplete statements about anger/guilt.

Procedure: Discuss with students that anger and guilt are very common feelings. When someone dies many people think that they or others were responsible for a death or could have prevented it. Statements like, "If only I had . . . " or "What if . . . " are common. Students may also be angry at other people (parent, sibling, teacher, others) for what they said and did or for what they did not say or do after the family member died. Many of the younger children at Fernside have been angry at the remaining parent because he or she could not prevent the death from occurring. One child felt the need to become physically stronger because his mother could not keep his father from dying. He thought that she would not be able to prevent him from dying either, so he had to be strong enough to defend himself.

Group Task: Place slips of paper with statements about anger and guilt in a small basket. Pass the basket around so that each child has an opportunity to pick one. The student reads the statement and fills in the blanks. Examples of statements are: I think I was most angry because . . . It made me furious when they said . . . I feel really mad at my ___ because. . . .

Closure: Discuss with students that they were not responsible for the death of the family member. Explore with students alternative ways to release the angry feelings that they may have.

Session Five: Nightmares and Dreams

Goal: To identify nightmares and dreams associated with being scared and related to the issue of security and safety needs.

Materials: Clay, the book *The Something*, paper, markers, and crayons.

Procedure: Introduce the topic by stating that some children have nightmares or dreams, or daydreams after the death of a loved one. Read the book, *The Something*, (Babbit, 1970) to generate discussion of the childrens' nightmares. Allow members to share their nightmares or dreams. Some children have had good dreams and this is a perfect time to allow them to talk about these or to question children about happy dreams.

Group Task: Give children modeling clay or drawing paper so that they can make representations of their nightmares or dreams.

Closure: Discuss ideas of confronting fears, ways of amending dreams, or making up their own dream scenarios.

Session Six: Summation of Feelings

Goals: Students identify that there are many feelings related to the death of a loved one and that these feelings ebb and flow.

Materials: Magazines, scissors, glue, posterboard, markers, and pens.

Procedures: Discuss the fact that we all have many feelings regarding the death of a loved one. Many of the feelings come and go, some days are happy and some are sad. This fluctuation in feelings is very normal for people who have had someone close to them die.

Group Task: Students are urged to make a collage of all of their feelings related to the death experience. A suggestion is to tell the students that they are going to explain what it felt like after their loved one died to a person who can't hear, but can see pictures and read words. The collages are then shared with the group.

Closure: This is the last session which deals with specific feelings. A summary of all of the feelings that the students have talked about would be appropriate.

Additional Sessions

After the sixth session the facilitators may want to survey the students to identify the future course of the group. Taking into consideration the noted themes and other suggestions for group sessions, the facilitators could establish an agenda for the following weekly sessions. Some possible avenues to explore include: returning to school after the death in regard to how the children were treated by teachers and students, cherished memories, individual accomplishments that have occurred after the death, things the children would like parents to know but are afraid to tell them, and how they have changed or the family has changed since the death.

Procedures to help facilitate the sessions could include excerpts from the book *Children Are Not Paper Dolls,* (Linn, 1982). This book would be especially helpful in discussing childrens' feelings about school and changes in the home environment. Encouraging the children to bring in pictures of the person who died or something memorable that belonged to the person is a wonderful way of stimulating conversation about memories. Making a treasure chest or memory book is another means of allowing the children to talk about the good memories they have of the person who died. Encouraging the children to help compose a newsletter is one way of helping them put into words the questions or concerns which they would like to discuss with parents.

At the final weekly session students should be asked to evaluate the group in terms of how it helped them understand their feelings, what they liked/disliked in regard to activities, if they would recommend the group to other children who had someone close to them die, what they would change about the group, and what they learned about themselves. An evaluation should also be sent home to the parent to assess if there had been changes in the child's behavior, what the child said about the groups, and if there was an increase in discussion about the death or the person who died.

Two other important activities should take place at the final meeting. There should be some discussion of the fact that it may be sad to have the groups end, even though students will be meeting every month. Ending the group is another loss issue. Reassure the students that the facilitators will be available at anytime, and that the students have formed a support network among themselves. The other issue is to affirm the childrens' involvement in the group. Having the students sign each others journals, or tell what they appreciated about each student can make the transition easier.

At some point, the weekly sessions may end and monthly follow-up meetings can be initiated. These meetings are generally less structured, in regard to format, than the weekly meetings. The main goals of the monthly meetings are to check on how each member is doing, to follow up on any concerns which had been raised in the weekly meetings, and to allow the children an opportunity to discuss any changes which have occurred in the home or school environment. This time together can be especially important for the child who has to face an anniversary date or special event where the absence of the person who died is painfully apparent.

Evidence for Effectiveness

Establishing grief groups for children is a new phenomena. Follow up studies on the children who have attended grief groups is an important piece of data that is missing from the literature. Fernside is just beginning to acquire such information. At this time, the data that have been accumulated consists of personal anecdotes regarding the positive affects of being involved in the groups. Children report that Fernside was fun, that it was a place to come to with other children who have experienced the same pain, that they could talk about the person who died without anyone making fun of them, that it helped to talk about all the feelings, and that they did not feel so different. Parents also have reported an increase in discussions at home and a reduction in the child's angry behavior.

A questionnaire was used at Fernside for the 1992 sessions and distributed to the children and the parents. The questionnaire was used to gather information on how frequently the respondent came to bimonthly sessions, if the sessions were perceived as helpful, identification of what was helpful, if coming to the groups helped in coping with any problems which occurred after the death, and suggestions for changes. Fifty-seven children responded to the questionnaire; and of that sample 93% felt that the groups had been helpful. The children reported that the leaders, the games and activities, the support, people listening, getting feelings out, talking about the person who died, and talking to someone other than family members helped the most. Forty-two parents responded to the questionnaire and 93% of those parents found the support groups to be helpful. The comments varied in regard to what was beneficial; however, the single element which was most often reported was that of a caring atmosphere where emotions and feelings could be released. The parents also commented on the fact that they could talk to their children more openly, and that it helped them feel less isolated as a family.

CONCLUSION

The literature suggests that unresolved grief can lead to major developmental barriers for children (Kubler-Ross 1975; Schneider, 1984). They may be at risk for losing the capacity to learn how to emotionally grow without overwhelming fears, nightmares, and guilt. Children may regress in terms of language, concentration, security and safety needs, and may have difficulty knowing when to express tears, anger, and fears. They may also erect barriers in order to resist discussions of death issues. Some children may not express their grief feelings at home because it makes a parent cry, or may not express feelings because they are frightened by their own emotions (guilt and anger). Adults need to realize that children feel guilty, withdraw from others, deny the occurrence of a death, and are angry. There is a need for adults to become aware of the nonverbal behavior which can reveal the child's internal feelings. Once adults understand the world of the grieving child, then they can help children name and claim feelings so that they can move ahead.

Grief groups can have a direct effect on the children in the group. They can also be viewed as indirect processes which effect the entire population of the school. By working with the teaching staff and the children in classrooms where a peer's loved one has died, the counselor, school psychologist, or other adults allow the taboo of talking about death to be lifted. Sanctioning children to talk about death issues helps to reduce their own individual fears and increases understanding of their own feelings.

The healing process is not a simple one. Too often the grieving child's needs are unmet due to myths about grief, dysfunctional support systems, and fear from other children and adults. The words of the children tell us, though, that they do grieve, they do understand, and they do hope for the future.

REFERENCES

Babbit, N. (1970). *The something*. Toronto, Canada: Collins Publishers.

Bowlby, J. (1969). *Attachment and loss: Attachment (Vol. I)*. New York: Basic Books.

Bowlby, J. (1973). *Attachment and loss: Separation, anxiety and anger (Vol II.)* New York: Basic Books.

Bowlby, J. (1980). *Attachment and loss: Loss, sadness and depression (Vol. III)*. New York: Basic Books.

Burrell, P. (1989, May). *Grief cycle*. Paper presented at the First Area Conference Concerning Grieving Children, Cincinnati, OH.

Cassini, K. K., & Rogers, J. L. (1985). *I want to help but I don't know how.* Cincinnati, OH: Grief Work of Cincinnati Inc.

Cassini, K. K., & Rogers, J. L. (1990). *Death and the classroom.* Cincinnati, Oh: Grief Work of Cincinnati Inc.

Clifton, L. (1983). *Everett Anderson's goodbye*. New York: Henry Holt and Company.

Engel, G. L. (1980). A group dynamics approach to teaching and learning about grief. *Omega: Journal of Death and Dying. 11*, 45-49.

Fassler, J. (1982). *My grandpa died today.* New York: Human Resources Press Inc.

Grollman, E. A. (1976). *Talking about death: A dialogue between parent and child.* Boston: Beacon Press.

Grollman, E. A. (1981). *Concerning death: A practical guide for the living.* Boston: Beacon Press.

Jackson, E. N. (1971). *When someone dies*. Philadelphia: Fortress Press.

Kremitz, J. (1981). *How it feels when a parent dies.* New York: Alfred Knopf, Inc.

Kubler-Ross, E. (1975). *Death: The final stage of growth.* Englewood Cliffs, NJ: Prentice-Hall.

LeShan, E. (1976). *Learning to say goodbye when a parent dies.* New York: Avon Books.

Lewis, B. G. (1991, December). Initiating bereavement support groups for children. *Communique, 20* (4), 6.

Linn, E. (1982). *Children are not paper dolls*. New York: The Publishers Mark.

Lord, J. H. (1990). *Death at school*. Dallas, TX: Mothers Against Drunk Driving.

Morganett, R. S. (1990). *Skills for living*. Champaign, Il: Research Press.

Prestine, J. S. (1987). *Someone special died*. Los Angeles: Price, Stern, Sloan Publishers Inc.

Rando, T. A. (1984). *Grief, dying and death: Clinical interventions for caregivers*. Champaign, IL: Research Press.

Rofes, E. (1985). *The kid's book about death and dying*. Boston: Little, Brown and Co.

Schneider, J. (1984). *Stress, loss, and grief*. Baltimore: University Park Press.

Worden, W. J. (1982). *Grief counseling and grief therapy*. New York: Springer Publishing.

Cognitive-Behavioral Groups for Children Manifesting ADHD and Other Disruptive Behavior Disorders

Lauren Braswell

North Psychology Clinic
Minnesota Competence Enhancement Project

SUMMARY. A model for school-based cognitive-behavioral groups for children manifesting symptoms of Attention-Deficit Hyperactivity Disorder (ADHD) and/or other disruptive behavior disorders is presented. Key aspects of organizational readiness to conduct this type of program are discussed, particularly the importance of having the support of the children's classroom teachers. The child group format and content, including recommended behavioral contingencies, are described. A brief review of the outcome literature concludes there is currently more justification for using this type of intervention with children manifesting disruptive behavior disorders other than ADHD or in addition to ADHD, and topics for future research are discussed.

Address correspondence to: Dr. Lauren Braswell, 5810 Northwood Ridge Road, Bloomington, MN 55437.

[Haworth co-indexing entry note]: "Cognitive-Behavioral Groups for Children Manifesting ADHD and Other Disruptive Behavior Disorders." Braswell, Lauren. Co-published simultaneously in *Special Services in the Schools* (The Haworth Press, Inc.) Vol. 8, No. 1, 1993, pp. 91-117; and: *Promoting Student Success Through Group Interventions* (ed: Joseph E. Zins, and Maurice J. Elias) The Haworth Press, Inc., 1993, pp. 91-117. Multiple copies of this article/chapter may be purchased from The Haworth Document Delivery Center [1-800-3-HAWORTH; 9:00 a.m. - 5:00 p.m. (EST)].

Many educators and mental health professionals believe that to consciously choose to conduct a group with 6 to 8 children displaying symptoms of Attention-Deficit Hyperactivity Disorder (ADHD) or other Disruptive Behavior Disorders is adequate grounds for questioning the sanity of the group leaders. This view may be correct. It is the purpose of this article, however, to inform readers about methods they could use if confronted with ADHD children who would appear to benefit from a positive therapeutic group experience.

In recent years, a number of different factors have contributed to a marked increase in efforts to develop and refine school-based intervention for children with ADHD. One factor involves greater awareness that possibly 3 to 5% of schoolaged children manifest ADHD and that the key symptoms of this disorder are chronic in nature (APA, 1987). In addition, long-term outcome studies have indicated that despite the dramatic short-term improvements achieved by treating some ADHD children with psychostimulant medication, the long-term prognosis of ADHD children treated via medication alone is no different than for those receiving no treatment (Weiss & Hechtman, 1986). In contrast, ADHD children who have received psychostimulant treatment along with multimodal interventions, that include educational interventions when needed, have achieved more positive outcomes (Satterfield, Satterfield, & Schell, 1987).

From a more pragmatic perspective, interest in school-based intervention for ADHD students has also increased as a result of a U.S. Department of Education (1991) memorandum clarifying that the special education needs of ADHD students are covered under the mandates outlined in Public Law 94-142, with these children most commonly served under the category of "Other Health Impaired." This policy clarification was an important step towards legitimizing the service needs of these children from the perspective of the school system and has made it easier for EBD/LD instructor time to be devoted to meeting their needs. For example, some EBD instructors have implemented programs such as the one described in this article as part of their service to these children.

The methods advocated in this article are based on a cognitive-behavioral approach to intervention that emphasizes performance-based practice, the use of developmentally appropriate behavioral contingencies, and the examination and possible modification of some of the child's (and his/her significant adults) thoughts, self-statements, beliefs, and/or expectancies. This approach assumes that while the primary symptoms of ADHD are difficult to ameliorate, it may be possible to help the child develop competencies that lower the risk for the emergence of serious secondary difficulties, such as low self-esteem, conduct problems, and/or poor peer relations. The current article provides an abbreviated description of the child group component and, due to space limitations, a very brief description of the teacher and parent intervention components recommended by Braswell and Bloomquist (1991). In contrast to past cognitive-behavioral efforts with impulsive and ADHD-type children, the Braswell and Bloomquist approach emphasizes group training to maximize opportunities for skills practice with peers, maintains a focus on specific social skills as well as problem-solving processes, and demands parent and teacher involvement in the training process. In addition, within the problem-solving training, the Braswell and Bloomquist curriculum places a great emphasis upon problem recognition/self-awareness training in light of the ADHD child's noted difficulties even recognizing when he or she is involved in a problematic situation.

TARGET POPULATION

The methods discussed in this article were developed for use with children displaying the primary symptoms of ADHD–inattention, impulsivity, and hyperactivity (Barkley, 1990). This condition is more commonly observed in boys than in girls. Symptoms are usually observable during the child's preschool years, but with the school environment's greater demand for self-control, the seriousness of the difficulties may not be apparent until school entry. In the classroom, such children are often observed to have difficulty sustaining attention to both schoolwork and social activities, to be highly distractible, and to blurt out comments at inappropriate times. Many of the children with these attentional difficulties are also noted to be quite fidgety and seem to be frequently out-of-seat; however, some children may manifest attentional difficulties in the absence of extreme motor activity. As a result of the primary symptoms or, perhaps, due to co-existing conditions, many ADHD children manifest conduct difficulties, social skills deficits, and learning disabilities. There is a particularly high degree of overlap between ADHD and other types of Disruptive Behavior Disorders, e.g., Oppositional Defiant Disorder (ODD) or Conduct Disorder (CD).

ADHD has been observed in children from all racial, cultural, and socioeconomic groups, at least as assessed in North American samples, but slight fluctuations across socioeconomic status (SES) have been observed. As discussed by Barkley (1990), rates are slightly elevated in lower SES samples and/or urban samples. Barkley (1990) speculates this observed difference could be the result of differential rates of pre- and perinatal difficulties, family instability, and/or downward "social drift" of ADHD individuals. Nonetheless, ADHD is generally considered an "equal opportunity problem."

Format

The current group methods have been carried out in several different formats within school environments. Most commonly, the training is structured as a "pull-out" group that includes children from several different classrooms and is conducted by the school psychologist, counselor, social worker, or special education staff. Such groups are structured to involve children of the same or approximately the same grade. When the group is conducted outside the classroom, the group leaders and relevant classroom teachers meet to exchange information about the skills addressed in group and to consider how to prompt and reinforce the use of these skills in the regular classroom setting. The program can also be adapted for use in resource room or self-contained classroom settings.

ORGANIZATIONAL READINESS

Given the importance of encouraging the child's skills use in the regular classroom setting, staff readiness for this program is crucial. In addition to having group leaders who are comfortable working with an active, demanding child population, the classroom teachers must be ready to create a classroom environment that invites children to assume a more active role in solving their own problems.

While some classroom teachers display immediate enthusiasm for this type of programming, others view it as, at best an inconvenience, and, at worst, as an obstruction to their goal of getting a particular child out of their classroom. In addition to the obvious step of having the entire faculty involved in deciding to implement this type of programming, securing staff support also requires strong endorsement of the program by the building administrator. It must be clear to all concerned that the principal values and supports the current effort and will look favorably upon positive teacher involvement in addressing the needs of the ADHD and/or ODD student. One concrete method for demonstrating such support involves the principal using the problem-solving methods trained in group as a format for resolving child and staff disputes that end up being addressed in his/her office. In another concrete display of support, this author knows of a principal who not only used these methods for conflict resolution but also served as one of the child group leaders.

Providing teachers with up-to-date information about ADHD and other disruptive behavior disorders is also important for overcoming dysfunctional attitudes that can interfere with productive action. Having accurate information can help some educators move beyond a stance of blaming of the child, parents, or themselves for the child's classroom difficulties and move toward greater recognition of the need for cooperative effort on the part of all involved with a given child. In particular, it may be important to stress that most ADHD children will spend the vast majority of their school day in regular education settings. Thus, it is to the teacher's advantage to be more prepared to cope with the behavior of these children.

Concerning the nature of teacher involvement, while teachers typically don't conduct the initial skills training, they must be prepared to prompt, encourage, and reinforce the child's efforts to use group-trained skills in the classroom. Prompting refers to the teacher taking an active role in pointing out good opportunities for the child to use his/her problem-solving skills. For example, the teacher can help the child recognize that situations such as a disorganized desk, confusion over a long-term project, interpersonal difficulties within a cooperative learning group, and/or problems getting homework completed and back to school are all excellent opportunities to use problem-solving. When the child uses problem solving appropriately, whether or not he was prompted to do so, it is extremely important that this effort be reinforced by the classroom teacher. The reader is referred to Braswell and Bloomquist (1991) for a detailed discussion of specific methods of prompting and reinforcing the child's use of problem-solving in the classroom.

To adequately inform teachers about their role in this training process it is recommended that the group leader or principal present the necessary information at a regular faculty meeting, at a special teacher assistance team meeting involving the teachers of children participating in group, or at some other specially reserved time prior to the beginning of group. Then, after the children have begun to display some skills mastery within group, the leader can ask the teachers to begin actively prompting and reinforcing skills use in the classroom. For example, the leader could ask to be on the agenda for a regular faculty meeting that occurs five to six weeks after the child group has begun. At such a meeting, it is particularly useful to have enough time to problem solve with the teachers about methods of encouraging more child skills use in the classroom. Ideally, group issues should become a semi-regular "agenda item" at subsequent faculty meetings to allow further coordination of group and classroom training efforts.

In addition to teacher involvement, the group leaders should plan some form of parental involvement in order to maximize potential group effectiveness. Three key methods of establishing this involvement include having the parents come to an information meeting about group, supplying them with problem-solving worksheets for home skills practice, and involving them in problem-solving about any inappropriate behaviors in group. The reader is referred to Braswell and Bloomquist (1991) for further discussion of this important issue.

PROCEDURES

Getting Started

Leader background. The individuals implementing the group should have previous children's group experience. Working with

ADHD children can be very challenging in a group context and one would not want to attempt to learn the basics of running a group and become accustomed to a new group curriculum with quite so demanding a clientele. . . . much like most of us would prefer to learn how to swim somewhere other than in the midst of roaring river rapids!

In addition to experience leading children's groups, experience with ADHD and/or ODD or CD children is also helpful in preparing the leader for the range of symptoms that may be presented. Finally, it is essential for the leaders to be trained in conducting cognitive-behavioral intervention with children manifesting disruptive behavior disorders or to have observed an experienced cognitive-behavioral therapist "in action" so many of the key concepts being presented in the current curriculum will be familiar to them.

As elaborated by Braswell and Bloomquist (1991), given the nature of this treatment, the group leader must be comfortable adopting an active, frequently didactic style, yet be capable of using this directive style to guide and prompt children to problem solve about their own dilemmas. The leader must be comfortable with the authoritative stance necessary to effectively implement the group's behavioral contingency system, yet able to side step power struggles and refrain from issuing verbal directives in those circumstances when it is more desirable for the children to both recognize and resolve their own behavioral issues in group.

Group composition. In terms of selecting children for group participation, both the child's cognitive level and symptomatology should be considered. Children should manifest a mental age of at least eight years and be capable of mastering concepts at a third grade level. The ideal candidate is the child who would seem to function more adaptively if he or she could only stop and think a bit more when faced with social or academic problem situations. Such children may manifest interpersonal difficulties related to their impulsive behavior and/or difficulties with anger management. They are often described as the kind of children who are easily "set-up" by other children to get in trouble with peers or adult authorities. The child who is capable of quietly scheming or setting up other kids is not considered an ideal candidate, for this type of child is already manifesting effective problem-solving skills but is using these skills in the service of anti-social goals.

The number and nature of the children participating in group should also be influenced by the number of group leaders. With one leader, the group should be limited to four children, especially if they are all extremely active and/or oppositional. With two leaders, such as an experienced leader and a trainee or volunteer, then the group size could be expanded to six challenging children or go as large as seven or eight if most of the children are not markedly oppositional. Whenever possible, the use of two leaders is strongly recommended.

Group Format

Across groups. The group curriculum is designed to be delivered in 45 to 55 minute sessions. Sessions are typically held weekly for 18 weeks or twice a week for a 9 week period. Because the curriculum is divided into distinct units, a shorter version of the program could be conducted by deleting selected units. It is recommended that a minimum of 12 sessions will be necessary to achieve a meaningful degree of content mastery, much less skills generalization, with an "average" ADHD child. When implementing all 18 sessions in a pull-out group format, sessions can be conducted weekly or some group leaders have stated a preference for conducting the first 9 to 12 sessions on a weekly basis and then moving to a biweekly format.

Within each group. After the initial group, the format to follow within each session is presented in Table 1. To summarize, the groups begin with a checking-in phase during which the children share important events of their week and discuss attempts to use group-trained skills. The group then learns and practices the social behavior goal for that session. The key session content is then presented, with accompanying role-playing, games and/or discussion. Following this phase, the points earned by group members are totaled and, as will be further discussed in the section on behavioral contingencies, the child earning the most points for that day earns the title of Kid for the Day (KFTD) and the privilege of picking the group's free time activity. Finally, the group engages in a relaxation period during which they share their reactions to that day's group.

Space limitations preclude a detailed discussion of all the possible methods of conducting relaxation training with these children,

TABLE 1. Child Group Format

1. CHECK-IN (10 minutes)–Each child discusses his/her week and attempts to apply program-related skills in extra-therapy environments. As group progresses and the children become more able to use their new skills, it is expected that check-in will take longer for each child (and that group members will have more opportunities to earn points for good listening while each member shares his/her week!)

2. SET SOCIAL BEHAVIOR GOALS (5 to 10 minutes)–After check-in, the therapists explain the social behavior goal to be practiced in that particular session (e.g. maintaining appropriate eye contact). While the therapists designate the goal behaviors in the early sessions, in later sessions the children can generate their own suggestions for behaviors to be practiced. The therapist's task is to describe and model the desired behavior. The children then receive points in the remainder of group for displaying the targeted behavior.

3. INTRODUCE NEW CONCEPT/SKILL (20 to 25 minutes)–The therapists present each new concept or skill via direct instruction, modeling, role-play exercises, and reinforced practice. It is assumed that much of this time will also be used to problem solve about ongoing group interactions.

4. KID FOR THE DAY DESIGNATION AND FREE TIME ACTIVITY (10 minutes)–At the end of each group, points are totaled. The child with the most points is designated "kid for the day" and he or she gets to select the free play activity for that day. The last 5 to 10 minutes of group are spent in that activity.

5. RELAXATION (5 minutes)–The therapist leads the group in simple tension releasing exercises. In later groups, group members may choose to lead the exercises.

6. REVIEW AND FEEDBACK (5 minutes)–Once the children appear to be relaxed, then the group members review the skills learned during that session, give constructive feedback to each other about behavior, and consider whether or not each child has attained the social behavior goal for that group.

but it should be noted that we tend to focus on brief muscle tension-release methods that are practical for the children to enact in other situations. Some groups have also enjoyed learning how to use deep breathing and self-calming talk to slow their pulse rates (see Braswell & Bloomquist, 1991, for additional discussion of this issue).

Group Content

Overview. Over the course of the 18 sessions, the children are introduced to a systematic method of talking themselves through problem situations. Table 2 presents both the social behavior goal and the key training content of each session. The five-step problem-solving model depicted in Figure 1 is presented and explained in sessions one through six. The sessions that follow then address application of this basic model to problems of interpersonal conflict, anger/frustration management, and effort management. The last three sessions are devoted to review and group termination issues.

While there are distinct content areas to be covered, no particular content domain is more important than conducting *in vivo* problem-solving about dilemmas occurring in group. The leaders should not put themselves under pressure to push through a certain amount of formal group content at the expense of helping the children learn to solve problems that matter to them. If one child is kicking the chair of another, that's a problem to be solved. If everyone is thirsty, that's a problem to be solved. If someone objects to an aspect of the behavioral contingency system, you get the idea.

Behavioral contingencies. In working with ADHD children it is *crucial* to employ contingencies that foster the learning and practice of key aspects of training content and that minimize the display of extremely disruptive behaviors. Given that contingencies are tools to serve learning, they should be modified in any circumstance in which it appears their use undermines rather than serves learning. Group leaders should tailor any system to make it ideally suited to their setting and target population, but the following system is described for the sake of example.

The heart of the recommended contingency system is a point system based upon the display of appropriate group behavior, the display of targeted social behavior goals, and the use of problem-solving to address dilemmas arising in group. The children are told they will earn points for following the group guidelines and for exhibiting the targeted social behavior. They can also lose points for violations of the group guidelines. In addition, they earn bonus points for engaging in good problem-solving if they are involved in a problem situation in group and double bonus points if they recognize any difficulty they might be creating for others and initiate problem-solving on their own. In other words, the behavioral contingency system reflects the high value placed on the display of adaptive problem-solving.

Why do the points matter to the children? While a number of different back-up rewards could be employed, one amazingly effective (and simple) reward is referred to as Kid for the Day (KFTD). Near the end of group, individual points are totaled and whoever has earned the most becomes the KFTD. This child has the privilege of selecting the free time activity for the group to engage in for the final 8 to 10 minutes of group. Typically, the leader presents three or four possible activities from which the KFTD selects his/her choice. Possibilities include various art activities, balloon volleyball, and variations on sports trivia games played in teams. To keep the contingency powerful, it is best to rotate the different choices of activities and periodically add in a mystery bonus reward, such as getting to have a small food treat while engaging in the activity.

Many groups are effectively managed with this point system; however, for highly disruptive groups, a strike system can also be added. This system is used to regulate extremely disruptive behavior such as physical aggression or very provocative namecalling. For any display of these extreme behaviors, the child receives a strike and if three strikes are received, he or she is out of group for a brief period. In some school settings, the group leader has prearranged with the principal that if a child acquires three strikes, then the consequence is that the child must meet with the principal to problem solve about his or her behavior and make a plan for engaging in more positive behavior back in group. If there are two leaders for the group, it is also possible for one of them to leave with the disruptive group member and, after a brief time-out period, engage the child in problem-solving about more effective management of his behavior in group. Still other leaders have worked out a system

TABLE 2. Training Content Overview

Session	Child Content (Social Behavior Goal)	Teacher/Parent
		Introduction to group content and goals
1	Introduction to Group	
2	Problem Recognition–external cues (eye contact)	
3	Problem Recognition–external and internal cues (eye contact)	
4	Problem Recognition–internal cues (expressing feelings appropriately)	
5	Generating Alternatives and Evaluating Consequences (expressing feelings appropriately)	
6	Reviewing Outcomes and Creating Back-up Plans (expressing feelings appropriately)	
7	Review	Begin prompting and reinforcing child's skill use in classroom and home environments
8	Interpersonal Problem-Solving I (sharing/cooperative behavior)	

Session	Child Content (Social Behavior Goal)	Teacher/Parent
9	Interpersonal Problem-Solving II (sharing/cooperative behavior)	
10	Anger/Frustration Management I (ignoring)	Continue to provide information to support adult efforts to prompt and reinforce skills use
11	Anger/Frustration Management II (ignoring)	Prepare adults for child attempts to use self-calming techniques
12	Anger/Frustration Management III (ignoring)	
13	Anger/Frustration Management IV (assertiveness)	
14	Poor Effort Management I (assertiveness)	Prepare adults for child attempts to problem-solve about boredom/poor effort situations
15	Poor Effort Management II (assertiveness)	
16	Program Review (group choice)	Generalization Planning
17	Program Review (group choice)	
18	Presentation and Celebration	Join children for session

FIGURE 1. Problem-Solving Visual Aide.

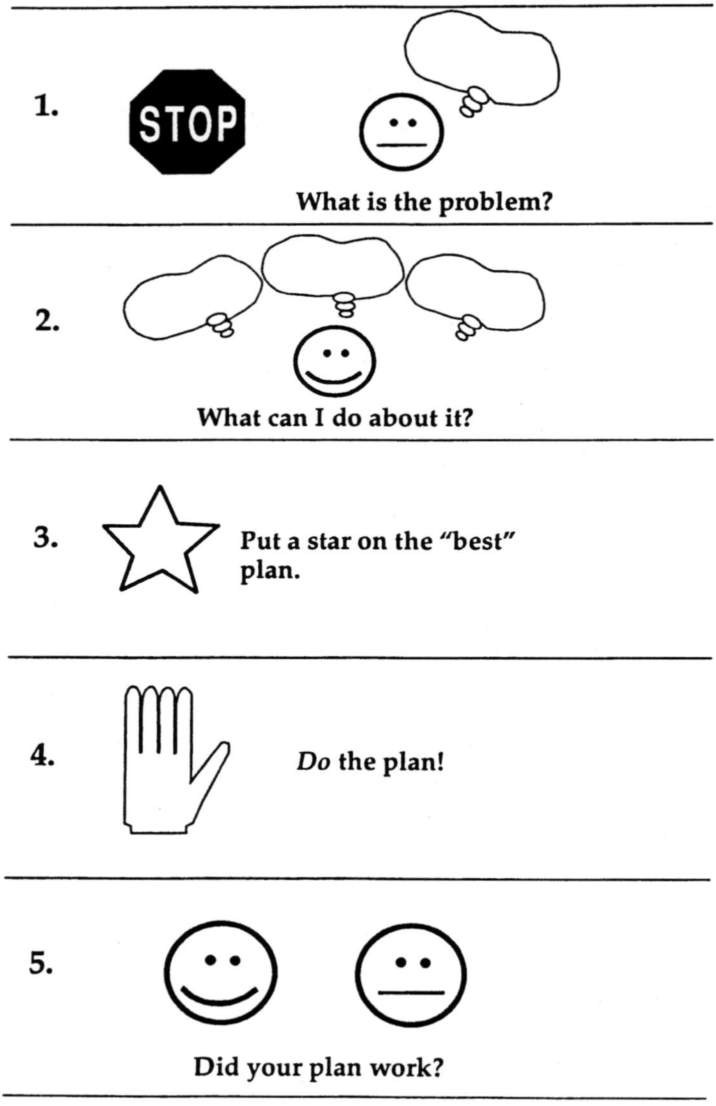

in which the parent is called if a child receives three strikes and the child and parent must problem solve about the situation. Needless to say different settings will require different back-up options.

In still other circumstances, leaders have found it valuable to add an effort-oriented contingency in which all children achieving at least a certain minimum point level earn an "effort point" for that session. Achieving a prearranged number of these effort points across sessions earns participation in some positive group activity, such as a pizza party or popcorn and video party. In this way, the appropriate effort of all children, not just the one earning KFTD, can be recognized.

Behavioral social skills goals. In addition to the content areas described in the next section, each session has a specific positive social behavior that the children can receive points for displaying. The specific behaviors emphasized with a particular group of children should be based on the behavioral needs of that group, but those listed in Table 2 represent common behavioral targets in the groups we have previously conducted. It is extremely important not to assume that the children understand the desired behavior. Rather, the leader must explain and model the desired social behavior. It is recommended that early groups focus on highly specific, relatively simple social behaviors, such as eye contact, and gradually move toward more challenging social behaviors, such as sharing or the appropriate use of ignoring, that will require greater discussion and modeling.

Introductory phase (Sessions 1-7). The first six or seven sessions provide an introduction to the problem-solving process. To provide the reader with a more fully elaborated picture of group, the first few sessions are described in great detail, while the activities of the later sessions are only briefly summarized. Those seeking more information about the later sessions are referred to Braswell and Bloomquist (1991).

The first session has a particularly full agenda, for the leader has the task of introducing the problem-solving steps, while also establishing group guidelines and an initial sense of group cohesion. In order to accomplish all of these important goals, it is suggested that the leader(s) first explain the purpose of the group and allow the children to introduce themselves. The leader can then ask the group to come up with guidelines to govern the behavior of all group members and explain that the group point system will, in large part, be tied to these group guidelines. Interestingly, it has been my experience that the leader will need to help the group refrain from being too strict and unrealistic in their expectations for their own group behavior. The leader will also need to be prepared to add and explain a guideline concerning confidentiality (e.g., "what others say in group, stays in group" or "no gossiping about group business"), as children are less likely to spontaneously offer this rule. Whenever possible, the leader should help the children reformulate a negatively worded rule into its positive alternative. For example, if the child says "No hitting," the leader could challenge the group to figure out what one should do instead of hit in certain situations and the rule might become "Keep your space" or "Use your words, instead of your body, to say what you feel."

After the guidelines have been established and written on a poster for display in the group room, the leader can explain the point system in greater detail. It is important for the children to know that, in addition to earning points for following the group guidelines, they can earn points for exhibiting the problem-solving skills that they will be practicing in group, especially when they need to problem solve about their own behavior. To aid the children's understanding, it is helpful if the leaders role play a situation in which a child did not participate in solving his/her own problem in group and then a situation in which the child's involvement in solving his or her own problem allowed him or her to earn extra points.

The leader then introduces a discussion of the potential value and power of self-talk. The group can be actively involved in this discussion by asking them to share helpful and not-so-helpful examples of how people talk to themselves. The leader may find it useful to ask the group how they think certain star athletes talk to themselves in crucial game situations. For example, the leader could ask, "When Michael Jordan has a chance to make a shot to put the Chicago Bulls ahead in the final seconds of the game, do you think he's saying 'I won't make it . . . I know I won't make it,' do you think he's thinking about what he's going to have for a snack after the game, or do you think he's thinking about exactly what he's got to do to make the shot?" After a few such examples, the leader can bring the discussion back to more relevant examples for the children by asking something like, "What about when a kid has to take a math test? Do you think the best way to begin the test is by telling himself 'I can't do this. I hate math?' Would it be best to be thinking about what he is going to do at recess, or would it be best to tell himself, 'Sure math's not my best subject, but I'm gonna go slowly and look at each problem one at a time so I can do my best.' " After some discussion about why the third choice is the best, the leader can move on to explain that the purpose of this group is to help the children understand what they can do and tell themselves to help things go better for them when they are working on their schoolwork or when they have to deal with problems that come up with other people, like friends, teachers, parents, and siblings.

The leader can then explain the use of the five step problem solving process when attempting to solve a variety of difficulties. It is helpful to give the children copies of Figure 1 and have the five steps written on a large poster or blackboard. If time permits, the group can then work through an example of how the five steps could be used with a lighthearted "problem" such as how to teach a cat to fly or turn pencil erasers into gold.

In the first group it is very important to allow adequate time to total group members points, designate a Kid for the Day, and have 7 to 10 minutes of free time. It must be clear to the children that their points do matter and will lead to a desired privilege. Thus, the group leader must fight the tendency to try to cram in too much content in the initial session and wait until the second session to even introduce the five steps if time is running short in the initial meeting.

In the second and third sessions, the group begins to address the complex issue of problem recognition. The second session begins with a review of the five problem-solving steps, with children earning points for being able to say the steps, with or without their problem-solving sheets in hand. The leader then explains the group will be learning more about the meaning of the first step of the problem-solving process, which involves being able to recognize the cues or signals that tell us a problem or challenging situation may be occurring.

With most groups, it is helpful to begin the discussion of problem recognition by focusing on external cues that a problem is occurring. This discussion can be introduced easily by asking the children what a stop light is and what are the meanings communicated by the different colors of a stoplight. Then ask the children to discuss the consequences of failing to attend to such signals. When working with 8 and 9 years olds, it may be helpful to discuss several other examples of common noninterpersonal signals, such as traffic signs, police or ambulance sirens, weather warning signals, etc., to be sure the children understand that the external world provides us with many important signals if we know how to interpret what they mean.

Once the concept of external noninterpersonal signals is clear, the group can move on to a discussion of external interpersonal signals. The group leader might say something like, "Just as stoplights give us signals that mean go, slow down, or stop, other people give us signals that may have similar meanings about our behavior. Can anyone show me what your teacher's face looks like when he or she is happy with what you are doing and wants you to keep doing that?" After several children have offered examples, ask them to figure out whether such signs of approval are like a red, green, or yellow light. After the group is clear that positive interpersonal cues are like green lights, then ask them how people show each other that they are not happy with the other's behavior. To structure this phase, ask each group member to show what his/her teacher or mother's face looks like just before the child is about to get in trouble for some type of misbehavior. Not surprisingly, many children can offer great impressions of the angry looks of their parents or teachers, even though they seem to be completely ignoring the signal value of such looks!

After this discussion phase, allow the children to address the concept of problem recognition in a more active manner. For example, the children can be engaged in "problem recognition charades" in which they pair up, decide on some type of interpersonal difficulty to act out without words, and then present this scenario to the group. The remaining group members must guess what is being acted out and describe the cues they used to determine what was occurring.

If time permits, the group can also discuss that humans have the ability to give each other cues through posture and tone of voice, as well as giving each other highly specific cues in the form of language/speech. Allow the children to model examples of body posture and tone of voice that tend to communicate different sorts of messages or intents. Again, rather than rushing this discussion, save this topic for next session if time in the second group is running short.

In the fourth session, the leader can continue to discuss interpersonal cues if necessary and then point out that we are constantly giving ourselves cues that have important information but we have to be able to understand what our bodies, feelings, and thoughts are telling us. Begin with asking the group how our bodies give us important signals. The children usually start off with examples of cues that indicate physical illness, hunger, thirst, needing to go the bathroom, etc. The group leader can praise these examples and then ask the children to describe how our bodies give us cues when we are worried or angry. This discussion is usually more difficult, so the children may need some help identifying signals such as flushed cheeks, racing heart beat, more rapid breathing, sweating palms, tense shoulders, etc. When conducting this discussion, it is helpful to give the children a drawing of a person and let them draw or color on this figure to illustrate potential bodily cues of anger or distress.

After discussing bodily cues, the group can then discuss feeling and thinking cues that also let us know when we are worried or angry or upset in some way. The reader is referred to Table 3 for an example. The process of clarifying the signal value of emotion for these children is important yet difficult, so the leader should certainly allow ample discussion and illustration time to assist the group's mastery of this concept. Adequate discussion of this notion sometimes requires two sessions. In addition, the notion of recognizing our internal cues is considered again in the later unit on anger and frustration management training.

The fifth and sixth sessions complete the initial introduction to the five step problem-solving process. By the fifth session, the group is usually ready to address concepts of generation of alternatives and evaluation of consequences. As elaborated in Braswell and Bloomquist (1991), this session involves teaching brainstorming and then the evaluation of possible solutions in terms of their advantages and disadvantages.

TABLE 3. Cues for Recognizing Anger/Frustration

Body Signals	Thought Signals	Action Signals
Increased breathing rate	"This is so dumb!"	Yell
Increased heart rate	"I hate myself!"	Cry
Increased sweating	"I hate you!"	Punch/hit/push
Flushed face	"I am dumb!"	Fidget
Tense muscles	"I want to hurt myself!"	Run
Loud voice	"I give up!"	Tremble
Intense voice tone	"I can't do anything right!"	Stare off into space
More body motion		

In session six, the group considers how to review the outcome of a selected choice to determine if it really was the best plan or if another idea should be tried. In those circumstances in which the selected choice did not produce the desired outcome or it proved to be difficult to implement due to some type of obstacle, children are trained to come up with a back-up plan. The leader can note that seemingly good choices for solving problems sometimes don't work for several reasons. In some situations, the other people involved refuse to cooperate with the selected choice, while at other times perhaps our own emotions and behaviors make it hard for us to implement the selected choice in an effective manner. When the child's emotional response or behavior is causing the problem, the back-up plan should involve some method through which the child can calm himself or get out of the upsetting situation in an appropriate way. When the problem involves another's behavior, the child may need to step back from the situation for a moment to come up with a new idea.

Sports analogies can be *very* helpful in getting across the need to come up with back-up plans and the need to step back from the situation in order to think clearly. For example, if a basketball team is having trouble running certain plays because of the defense of the other team, ask the group "Do the players just give up? No, they try another kind of play or ask for a time-out to make new plans."

After covering the content described above, it is helpful to take a session to review what it means to engage in problem recognition, alternative generation, consideration of consequences, review of outcomes, and the creation of back-up plans. In this session it may also be desirable to allow the group to earn extra activity time by actively and appropriately participating in the review process.

Application with specific content areas (Sessions 7-15). After the steps of the problem-solving process have been explained in some detail, the group then devotes a couple of sessions to focusing on how these methods can be applied with interpersonal problems or dilemmas. Interpersonal perspective-taking or putting yourself in the other guy's shoes is the central concept introduced in this unit. These sessions involve a great deal of role-playing in which the children have the opportunity of switching roles so they can practice looking at the same situation from a variety of perspectives.

The next unit focuses on anger/frustration management by combining the five step problem-solving process with stress inoculation training methods developed for use with adults by Novaco (1978) and modified for use with disruptive children by Lochman, Nelson, and Sims (1981). The stress inoculation approach emphasizes helping individuals identify their personal cues of arousal, teaching some arousal coping methods, and practicing the use of these methods in increasingly stressful situations.

Effort management is addressed in Sessions 14 and 15. Discussion of this issue usually begins with helping the children recognize how much they are bothered by lack of effort on the part of others and, in turn, to recognize how their lack of effort might affect those close to them. The next step in effort management involves helping the children identify the physiological cues, behaviors, feelings, and thoughts that often accompany or precede poor effort. Finally, the children are asked to brainstorm ideas for what to do when they recognize feelings of boredom or frustration in relation to a particular task. The key point for the children to grasp is that feeling bored or frustrated is a predictable event and there might be some things they could do to manage those feelings that are more adaptive than the behaviors they have been using to cope with such emotions.

Final review (Sessions 16-18). The final sessions allow the leader to adequately review previously presented skills. One method of conducting this review process that is often appealing to the children involves working together to create a "problem-solving movie" that will be shared with other school personnel. To create such a movie, each individual in the group is allowed to select a problem he or she has struggled with in real life and act out what happens when he or she does not do good problem solving in this situation, then act out a contrasting example of how this situation could be handled with good problem solving. The "star" of a particular scene gets to select group members to co-star in his or her movie or in small groups it may be possible to use all group members in every scene. The group should also decide whom to invite to the "screening" of their movie, e. g., classroom teachers, principal, school social worker, etc., and create invitations for these guests. Depending upon the limits of the training environment, the group can also problem solve about whether or not to serve refreshments at the screening of the movie and how these refreshments should be provided. Preparing and videotaping the movie usually requires two sessions, with the movie being shown in the final group session. In this final session, it also works well to begin group with the regular check-in phase and explanation of the social behavior goal, so guests can get a little taste of the regular group activities. To increase the probability of having a productive final session, the leader could choose to continue the behavioral contingency system, perhaps with children and guests alike earning points for good group behavior and participating in the final free time activity.

GROUP SPACE AND MATERIALS

To run an effective group it is ideal to use a room that is a third to a half the size of a regular classroom. Such space is not so large as to encourage uninhibited flight around the room or so small that it precipitates otherwise unnecessary physical conflicts. In addition to the leaders having a therapist manual (see Braswell & Bloomquist, 1991), it is helpful to have construction paper and posterboard available for some of the group tasks. To aide generalization to the classroom setting, it can be useful to make problem-solving posters similar to the design depicted in Figure 1 and have teachers display these posters in their classrooms. Finally, the leaders need to have materials necessary for activity choices for the final 10 minutes of group.

METHODS OF ASSESSING OUTCOME

For assessing the outcome of group participation, we recommend a combination of normative and ideographic measures gathered from both the child and his/her teachers and parents.

At the most basic level, the leader can administer an informational exam to document that the information presented in group has, in fact, been learned, whether or not it is being appropriately applied. Such an exam could ask the child to list the problem-solving steps, identify common signals of anger/frustration, describe one or two methods for relaxing tense muscle, etc.

Selected parent and teacher rating scales and child self-report measures that might be appropriate for pre- and post-group assessments are listed in Table 4. Leader-developed scales that allow the teacher to rate each child on two or three individualized goals can also be helpful in documenting progress (or the lack thereof). Rating scales that simply list common ADHD symptoms, such as inattentiveness, distractibity, impulsivity, etc., are unlikely to reflect change in this context, for the treatment doesn't target the child's symptoms *per se* but rather seeks to help

TABLE 4. Selected Child, Parent and Teacher Rating Scales

Child Self-Report

Children's Action Tendency Scale (Deluty, 1979)

Children's Problem-solving Measure (Bloomquist, Anderson, Cohen, Hopwood, & Everhart, 1991)

Parent and Teacher Measures

Home and School Situations Questionnaire (Barkley, 1990)

Problem-Solving Rating Scale–Parent and Teacher versions (Bloomquist & Wilson, 1991)

Scale of Social Competence and School Adjustment (Walker & McConnell, 1988)

Self-Control Rating Scale (Kendall & Wilcox, 1979)

the child cope with the difficulties arising from these symptoms. Sociometrics, behavioral analogues, and direct observation of classroom behavior are all excellent assessment methods; however, they may not be practical for the typical school professional to conduct on an ongoing basis.

RATIONALE

While the need for effective treatments with this population is easy to document, clarifying the value of specific methods with specific populations has been a more difficult pursuit. As discussed by Kendall and Braswell (in press), many cognitive-behavioral efforts have achieved success with school-based samples of children presenting with some of the symptoms of ADHD and/or other disruptive behavior disorders. When examining treatment samples that include only children manifesting clinically significant levels of ADHD, however, the results of cognitive-behavioral efforts have been much less impressive. Only in studies in which the cognitive-behavioral training addressed anger coping strategies or behavioral self-monitoring training have there been some suggestions of positive impact (Hinshaw, Whalen, & Henker, 1984a, 1984b). In contrast, despite the recognition of how difficult it is to treat conduct disordered children, cognitive-behavioral group interventions have been able to achieve clinically meaningful and, in some cases, durable treatment effects with this population (Kazdin, Bass, Siegel, & Thomas, 1989; Kendall, Reber, McLeer, Epps, & Ronan, 1990; Kolko, Loar, & Sturnick, 1990; Lochman, 1991). These findings seem puzzling, particularly in light of the previously noted diagnostic overlap among and between the ADHD, ODD, and CD populations. Kendall and Braswell (in press) have speculated that cognitive-behavioral methods may be most appropriate when focused on issues such as coping with anger-inducing situations. The feasibility and efficacy of comprehensive, school-based cognitive-behavioral treatment for children with ADHD and other disruptive behavior disorders is currently being evaluated through the Minnesota Competence Enhancement Project (August, Bloomquist, Ostrander & Braswell, 1990).

FUTURE DIRECTIONS

In addition to remaining questions about the usefulness of cognitive-behavioral therapy with ADHD children, there are a number of concerns that merit much more intense investigation. Two issues of particular interest to this author include generalization training and recognition of the implications of this approach as they relate to the child's broader environment.

Training for generalization back to the classroom is a key concern of any school-based intervention. The current program attempts to address this issue by conducting training in a peer context and through formal involvement of the teacher and parent in the training process; however, there are many questions remaining about how much teacher/parent involvement is necessary to achieve an adequate level of skills transfer and about the level of prompting and reinforcement necessary to assure skills maintenance. Determining the staff and/or materials supports needed to help the classroom teacher implement the prompting and reinforcement is a related concern.

A greater understanding of the interplay of cultural/environmental concerns and the implicit assumptions of this type of intervention is also important. For example, the cognitive problem-solving approach implies that it is desirable to be reflective in one's mode of response to a challenge or dilemma. While this assumption may be generally true for most people, it poses a potential conflict for children whose school environment demands reflective behavior but whose neighborhood and/or home environment is more reinforcing of an "act first-think later" orientation. For children residing in high crime areas, being "too reflective" before responding in some circumstances might put them at risk for bodily harm. As a mother once shared with me, "This stuff is fine for the classroom, but my boy has also got to know how to act on the street." Her words echo the concerns of Whalen and Henker (1987) who, among other issues, emphasize the need for cognitive-behavioral training to do a better job of helping children discriminate between situations in which it makes sense to reflective and situations in which a rapid, intuitive response is more adaptive.

Through a better understanding of the impact of both "macro" systems issues, such as cultural environment, and more "micro" concerns, such as generalization training strategies, the field may yet produce a feasible and effective approach to serving ADHD children through school-based programming.

REFERENCES

American Psychiatric Association. (1987). *Diagnostic and statistical manual of mental disorders* (3rd ed., rev.). Washington, DC: Author.

Barkley, R. A. (1990). *Attention Deficit Hyperactivity Disorder: A handbook for diagnosis and treatment*. New York: Guilford.

Bloomquist, M. L., Anderson, D., Cohen, C., Hopwood, J., & Everhart, K. (1991). *Measure of children's problem-solving*. Unpublished manuscript, University of Minnesota.

Bloomquist, M. L., & Wilson, M. (1991). *Problem-solving rating scale–parent and teacher versions*. Unpublished manuscript, University of Minnesota.

Braswell, L. & Bloomquist, M. L. (1991). *Cognitive-behavioral therapy with ADHD children: Child, family and school interventions*. New York: Guilford.

Deluty, R. H. (1979). Children's Action Tendency Scale: A self-report measure of aggressiveness, assertiveness, and submissiveness in children. *Journal of Consulting and Clinical Psychology, 47*, 1061-1071.

Dodge, K. A. (1986). A social information processing model of social competence in children. In M. Perlmutter (Ed.), *Cognitive perspective on children's social and behavioral development* (pp. 77-125). Hillsdale, NJ: Erlbaum.

Dodge, K. A., Murphy, R. R., & Buchsbaum, K. C. (1984). The assessment of intention-cue detection skills in children: Implications for developmental psychology. *Child Development, 55*, 163-173.

Kazdin, A. E., Bass, D., Siegel, T., & Thomas, C. (1989). Cognitive-behavioral therapy of children referred for antisocial behavior. *Journal of Consulting and Clinical Psychology, 57*, 522-535.

Kendall, P. C., & Braswell, L. (in press). *Cognitive-behavioral therapy with impulsive children* (2nd ed.). New York: Guilford.

Kendall, P. C., Reber, M., McLeer, S., Epps, J., & Ronan, K. R. (1990). Cognitive-behavioral treatment of conduct-disordered children. *Cognitive Therapy and Research, 14*, 279-297.

Kendall, P. C., & Wilcox, L. E. (1979). Self-control in children: Development of a rating scale. *Journal of Consulting and Clinical Psychology, 47*, 1020-1029.

Kolko, D. J., Loar, L. L., & Sturnick, D. (1990). Inpatient social-cognitive skills training groups with conduct disordered and attention deficit disordered children. *Journal of Child Psychology and Psychiatry, 31*, 737-748.

Lochman, J. E. (1992). Cognitive-behavioral intervention with aggressive boys: Three year follow-up and preventive effects. *Journal of Consulting and Clinical Psychology, 60*, 426-432.

Lochman, J. E., Nelson, W. M. III, & Sims, J. P. (1981). A cognitive-behavioral program for use with aggressive children. *Journal of Clinical Child Psychology, 10*, 146-148.

Novaco, R. (1978). Anger and coping with stress: Cognitive-behavioral Interventions. In J. Foreyt & D. Rathjen (Eds.), *Cognitive-behavior therapy: Research and application* (pp. 135-173). New York: Plenum.

Satterfield, J. H., Satterfield, B. T., & Schell, A. M. (1987). Therapeutic interventions to prevent delinquency in hyperactive boys. *Archives of General Psychiatry, 26*, 56-64.

United States Department of Education. (September, 1991). *Memorandum on the subject of clarification of policy to address the needs of children with Attention Deficit Disorder within general and/or special education*. Washington, DC: Author.

Walker, H. M., & McConnell, S. (1988). *The Scale of Social Competence and School Adjustment*. Austin, TX: Pro-Ed.

Weiss, G., & Hechtman, L. T. (1986). *Hyperactive children grown up: Empirical findings and theoretical considerations*. New York: Guilford.

The Power of Positive Peer Influence: Leadership Training for Today's Teens

Sharon Rose Powell

Princeton (NJ) Center for Leadership Training

SUMMARY. The Peer Group Connection (PGC) is a primary prevention program that enlists the power of peer influence to help teenagers cope with the universal, everyday problems and pressures of becoming adults. It addresses important transitions in young people's lives by building into schools an important set of rituals and practices that reinforce healthy values in students and encourage critical thinking.

PGC offers a variety of large and small group experiences that create a special bond among peers. This kind of team-building is the essential foundation of a strong, diverse, and democratic society.

Those of us who work with adolescents are acutely aware of young people's urgent need to be accepted by their peers and to be members of a group that both supports and reinforces their personal identity at a time of life when physical and emotional changes can

---

Address correspondence to: Dr. Sharon Rose Powell, President, Princeton Center for Leadership Training, Princeton Pike Corporate Center, Building 3, 997 Lenox Drive, Suite 304, Lawrenceville, NJ 08648-2317.

[Haworth co-indexing entry note]: "The Power of Positive Peer Influence: Leadership Training for Today's Teens." Powell, Sharon Rose. Co-published simultaneously in *Special Services in the Schools* (The Haworth Press, Inc.) Vol. 8, No. 1, 1993, pp. 119-136; and: *Promoting Student Success Through Group Interventions* (ed: Joseph E. Zins, and Maurice J. Elias) The Haworth Press, Inc., 1993, pp. 119-136. Multiple copies of this article/chapter may be purchased from The Haworth Document Delivery Center [1-800-3-HAWORTH; 9:00 a.m. - 5:00 p.m. (EST)].

affect self-esteem. When rapid and fundamental change is also occurring in society at large, as it is in the 1990s, the personal stresses of moving from childhood to adulthood are compounded. In addition to the common anxieties and fears that adolescents experience, substantial numbers of teenagers are affected by the more devastating consequences of dropping out of school, teenage pregnancy, sexually transmitted disease, drug addiction, homicide, and suicide (Feldman & Elliott, 1990).

It is far more difficult for teens to draw strength from the family and community when both are being defined in new ways. In such turbulent times, the parental and communal stability that traditionally support a child's development can no longer be taken for granted; in too many cases, they simply do not exist. In suburbs and inner cities, even in our idealized rural and small-town America, children are beset by pressures. Is it any wonder, then, that the adolescent's need to be part of a group of peers is more urgent than ever?

The adolescent's need to be accepted and recognized by peers can affect feelings of security, perceptions of importance, and independent decision-making (Silber, 1961). The transition from eighth grade into a new and often impersonal high school can be a particularly vulnerable time for young people. Unless entering high school students have the good fortune to participate on an athletic team or belong to a singing or theater ensemble, they are unlikely to experience an initial sense of connectedness to their peers or to the school as a whole.

It is the responsibility of those of us who work in schools to insure that all children experience the value of being on a team and of making worthy contributions to others. It behooves us as adults to channel peer influence in positive ways and to utilize the powerful effects that young people can have on one another by encouraging activities in school that promote student leadership, team building, and community service.

These are precisely the goals of the Princeton Center for Leadership Training, a private not-for-profit organization that designs and conducts leadership training programs in schools and other educational institutions. Its mission is to improve the opportunities for young people to succeed in school and in life by helping them develop their leadership skills and by training teams of educators, parents, and interested community adults to work collaboratively to create a positive and supportive education environment.

The mission of the organization stems from a number of fundamental beliefs and principles:

- Leadership is the ability to work effectively in a group, to make a positive contribution to the group process and to stimulate and motivate others to function as a team, as well as to achieve common objectives and solve common problems.
- It is essential to establish and cultivate leadership skills in young people so that they can mature as leaders for the future.
- Collaboration among similar and diverse groups is essential for any organization or education institution to create positive, lasting change and a supportive learning environment.
- The inclusion of leadership skills in the process of changing and advancing education systems will result in improved education communities and better prepared students.

BACKGROUND

Mental health specialists for decades have agreed that the happiness and adjustment of young people depends significantly on the development of peer group relationships (Mechem, 1943). The American high school has been the primary setting in which adolescent peer groups operate, but systematic use of peer groups to influence adolescent development is a relatively recent phenomenon. Teachers and counselors have traditionally been recognized as role models for children, but the role of students as peer helpers and facilitators has been overlooked (Hamburg & Varenhorst, 1972).

Educators alone cannot face the challenge of helping adolescents cope with today's problems. Research shows that the most successful prevention models in schools utilize older peers to influence or help their younger peers, serving as tutors, mentors, and peer leaders (Dryfoos, 1990).

Problems such as school violence, drug abuse, and racism are concerns that adults must share with today's teenagers. By sharing roles of authority and leadership with young adults, we can create a more caring and safe school community in which all of us can live and learn together effectively.

When considering peer leadership programs, it is first important to examine the concept of "leadership training." What constitutes leadership? Can you train people to be leaders? Leaders, it is often said, are born, not made. While there is no denying the fact that some people seem to have an innate talent for leadership, it is also true that talent can be developed–and that *leadership skills can be learned* by those who might never imagine themselves playing such a prominent role in the world.

Leaders come from every ethnic, cultural, religious, and socio-economic background. They are male and female, old and young, and every age in between. The key to their leadership is not to be found in some ascriptive norm, as the sociologists call those traits we are born with, but rather in descriptive or acquired traits, in this case, the ability to inspire and motivate others to dedicate time and energy towards the achievement of goals (Gardner, 1990).

Obviously, there are as many styles of leadership as there are leaders. One well-known model is the authoritarian leader who defines goals and makes decisions, telling people what to do without first consulting them about their needs and expectations. At the other end of the continuum is the person in a responsible position who does not want to dictate but has difficulty accomplishing goals, in part because goals are not clearly defined and the leader has not paid attention to the *process* required to achieve them, and in part because he or she does not know how to work cooperatively with others in groups.

Neither of these leadership models is effective, especially in the context of an effort to change education in America: the first is too authoritarian, the second is too diffuse and untutored in the fundamentals of communications and group dynamics. Neither takes advantage of the process or opportunities of shared decision-making. The Princeton Center's training programs give leaders the skills they need not merely to avoid both extremes, but to become inspirers, mobilizers, and practitioners of positive change. The goal is to create a caring learning environment, where students and educators alike work cooperatively. It is a program that uses John Dewey's learning-by-doing approach to develop a commitment to learning that will last a lifetime. Only that kind of commitment will prepare students to succeed in a world where every kind of change–social, economic, political, technological, and scientific–is rapid and far-reaching.

PEER LEADERSHIP TRAINING

All of the Princeton Center's leadership training programs–whether for educators, parents, or students–focus on communications and group dynamics, the fundamental skills required by those who wish to succeed in today's world. The Peer Group Connection (PGC) is a peer leadership training program that trains educators to work with high school seniors who in turn serve as role models and mentors to groups of incoming students.[1] Teams of educators participate in leadership training conferences conducted by the Princeton Center, and these teachers pass along the new skills they have acquired to student peer leaders in a year-long for-credit course that is an integral part of the school curriculum.

The Peer Group Connection places students in a key role within their schools, one where they share responsibility for the welfare of their younger peers and can use their powerful influence as role models to contribute to a climate of mutual respect and support. This important responsibility requires a serious commitment of time and study: participants must learn the skills of co-leader facilitation and effective group management, practice shared decision-making and learn the tools of individual and group assessment.

GOALS AND OBJECTIVES OF THE PROGRAM

The Princeton Center has developed a leadership training program that emphasizes three important goals:

---

1. Correspondence about the Peer Group Connection program should be directed to the Princeton Center for Leadership Training, 997 Lenox Drive, Suite 304, Lawrenceville, NJ 08648-2317. A modified version of the Peer Group Connection program for high schools has been introduced in middle schools in Atlanta, Georgia, South Central Los Angeles, and Trenton, New Jersey.

1. To build caring, safe, and effective learning communities where ethnic, racial, and cultural differences are respected;
2. To motivate students to stay in school, improve their academic performance, and develop a lifelong commitment to learning; and
3. To develop leadership skills among educators and students so that they can work cooperatively for positive change in their school communities.

PGC succeeds in schools where teachers are willing to become learners and where they encourage a process whereby students become teachers of themselves and of others. PGC succeeds when educators and students are willing to pass along their skills in communications and group dynamics to ever-broader segments of the school community, not feeling threatened by competition from those who also acquire high-level skills, but instead celebrating the accomplishments of others which benefit everyone who participates in the group process. More specifically, the Peer Group Connection program has four objectives towards which measurable progress is made:

1. Increasing participants' *competence* as members and/or leaders of groups. A fundamental assumption is that leaders play a variety of roles during the course of a group's existence: facilitator, summarizer, clarifier, to name but a few. Moreover, every member of any group assumes one or more of these roles, permanently or intermittently, and therefore each participant functions as a co-leader of the group. The Princeton Center's training teaches educators and students how to observe their own behavior and that of others, how to identify the roles members take on in groups, and how to become more aware of the effects of that behavior on the group. Communication skills are very much a part of this process. Participants learn how to ask thoughtful questions that prompt critical thinking and how to listen actively to what other members of the group are saying.
2. Increasing participants' *confidence* in their ability to act as leaders. Competence without confidence is inadequate to the task of bringing about change. The Princeton Center's training

provides a supportive environment in which each group member can risk trying new leadership roles while receiving the kind of feedback that promotes personal growth. In this context, shy young people, for example, can become negotiators instead of non-participating observers, and domineering people can practice being supporters.

3. Increasing participants' sense of *connectedness* to other members of the group. Confidence develops when each member of a group enjoys a feeling of belonging, when each is assured that his or her contribution towards achieving the group's objectives is valued. Again, the training provided by the Princeton Center is experiential. Educators and students spend time practicing the arts of sharing roles and responsibilities and of giving and getting support.
4. Increasing participants' *understanding* of group dynamics, that is, how groups come together and what happens during the five-stage group cycle of development (Stanford, 1977). An understanding of group stages is key to the design and implementation of the Peer Group Connection program. The Princeton Center's leadership training not only teaches educators and students what can be done to move a group from one stage to another as it progresses towards success; it also allows enough time for them to *practice* the skills required to communicate effectively with others and to participate in groups at all stages of their existence.

PROGRAM DESCRIPTION

Given the breadth and depth of the problems that are said to plague our schools, especially high schools, it is no wonder that educators and their critics occasionally fall prey to programs that promise quick and total remedies. The Peer Group Connection makes no such claims. Nor does it assume that there is nothing right about our schools. On the contrary, it recognizes that much that is happening is good, that educators and their students are struggling to cope with virtually unprecedented problems in families and society, and that we can build on our successes while learning from our failures. Using this knowledge can help us determine what must change and how to accomplish that change.

Training in communications and group dynamics takes time, too, because PGC seeks to create certain kinds of leaders who commit themselves to their own growth as well as that of others. It is important to explore together those new styles of leadership which will be effective for a very diverse world. (Theobald, 1986)

That kind of leadership style comes naturally to only a few; the rest of us can learn how to do it however.

The establishment of PGC begins with an in-service day during which administrators, faculty, and staff are introduced to the program and to its philosophy. The PGC program works best when a team of three faculty work with and train a class of 12-14 senior peer leaders who, in turn, run small-group activities each week that reach approximately 100 incoming students. To reach larger numbers of students, two additional faculty can be added for every peer leadership class of 14 seniors who work with another 100 first year students.

TEACHER SELECTION AND TRAINING

A team of three faculty, a PGC coordinator and two advisors, are selected by their high school principal to run the program. Faculty teams should represent the diversity of their school's student population, have a good rapport with their students, and be open, flexible, and well-organized. These newly-selected PGC teams join teachers and counselors from other urban and suburban, public and private schools for an intensive four-day training conference conducted by Princeton Center staff. This exhilarating and demanding program begins at 8:30 a.m. and ends at 10:00 p.m. each day and includes time to experience PGC activities firsthand and to discuss, practice, and reflect on personal learning and group observations.

The four-day conference is followed by two all-day training workshops and two on-site visits by Princeton Center staff who observe the PGC program in operation, help team members evaluate its effectiveness, and suggest ways to improve it. The entire process includes another four-day conference and two one-day follow-up workshops during the second year of training, when more advanced skills in communications and group dynamics are taught and practiced by PGC coordinators and advisors.

Training conferences include sessions on the Peer Group Connection program itself, so that the members of each school's faculty team become thoroughly familiar with its purposes, learn the logistics of establishing the program in their school, practice using the activities described in the Peer Group Handbook (Powell, 1988), and develop the competence and confidence to adapt and augment those activities as appropriate to their own students' needs. The PGC faculty team also learns how to work together to supervise not only the peer leaders, but also the large number of incoming students who participate in the program. The team of faculty will learn how to become role models for their students, demonstrating by their own behavior the skills and responsibilities of co-leadership and the kind of commitment to cooperative, lifelong learning that is essential in a rapidly-changing world. Because they are themselves a leadership team with complementary strengths, they are comfortable with the idea of taking on different leadership roles, and with allowing students to be leaders, too. It is strongly recommended that no single teacher run the program. Instead, teachers who work as a team serve as role models for a program that is built around the insight that peer groups are effective teaching and learning resources for today's adolescents.

STUDENT LEADER TRAINING

During the two-year training period, the school's PGC faculty team works directly with peer leaders, who have been carefully selected to represent the diverse groups within the student population. Students interested in participating in the program must apply in the spring of their junior year in high school; invariably, there are many more applicants than places. As part of the application process, students answer essay questions about how they could contribute to the program and what they expect to gain from the experience. In addition, applicants participate in group problem-solving interviews where they are asked to discuss hypothetical peer-related problems and to demonstrate solutions in skits where they assume appropriate roles.

Those students who are selected should, as a group, include an equal number of young men and women who participate in a variety of extracurricular activities and who come from ethnically and racially diverse backgrounds. Selected students should also have demonstrated that they are responsible and caring individuals who can serve as positive role models for their peers. It is important that this group include students who have clearly demonstrated their capability as leaders but who have never been in leadership positions within the school. In this way, many more students will have opportunities to experience leadership than was previously possible before PGC.

The student peer leaders make a commitment to attend training classes five days each week in an elective, year-long for-credit course that begins with a three-day retreat held at the end of summer. During this retreat, their training emphasizes creating an atmosphere of support and trust, essential to group cohesiveness. Through a series of carefully-designed games and exercises, the peer leaders become acquainted with each other and learn how to cooperate in a group. They examine and express their ideas on a variety of topics related to PGC, learning how to become active listeners and to give constructive feedback to others in the group. They learn how to develop their own behavioral objectives and how to measure the attainment of these goals through individual and group analysis.

An important aspect of the training includes an introduction to the concept of group stages and then frequent opportunity to experience these stages firsthand. The five stages of groups (Bion, 1961) include:

Stage 1: Forming

Group members define the purpose for which they have come together, while paying attention to getting to know each other, assessing their own and others' strengths and limitations, and establishing what they have in common.

Stage 2: Norming

During this stage, the group establishes the ground rules for its work. These mutually agreed upon guidelines include creating group rituals and healthy practices that promote development of self-discipline and the sense of belonging to a team engaged in a worthy enterprise.

Stage 3: Storming

A critical stage in the group cycle is the inevitable moment when differing visions of the nature of the problem and the preferred solutions give rise to stalemate, conflict, and a sense of chaos or futility. At this point, groups are most in danger of failing because unhealthy practices such as scapegoating, denial, or polarization can impede progress towards achieving the goals defined in Stage 1, and can un-do the group cohesion developed in Stage 2. The Princeton Center's training will help people to recognize "storming," to stop and analyze the particular form it is taking, and to engage in a process that helps the group move on to the next stage in the group cycle.

Stage 4: Performing

During this stage, each group member develops a personal stake in the achievement of the group's objectives. Each understands his or her responsibilities as a co-leader and recognizes the value of every member's contribution. Consensus (not necessarily unanimity) is achieved, and the end of the group's existence is in sight. Its goals–short-term and/or long-term–are accomplished.

Stage 5: Mourning/Morning

Every group ends, sometimes in the sense that its task is finished and its members disperse, sometimes because a new group forms with new members and different objectives. In either case, however, the group must prepare for the time when the close relationships members have established with each other will be changed. During this stage, group members should spend time on assessment of the project and their contributions to it, on focused reflection, and on preparation for new beginnings as members of different groups.

This theoretical knowledge of group stages helps leaders to anticipate the concerns that members may have at different stages of development, the breakdowns in group cohesion and productivity that are likely to occur, and the needed roles and interventions that are required for leaders to be effective in groups.

Finally, peer leaders organize themselves into teams comprised of two people who have not been close friends prior to their participation in PGC and learn how to work cooperatively, sharing responsibilities for running small-group discussions. Whenever possible, it is best to have co-leader teams comprised of one male and one female. This is one of the rare opportunities for students of the opposite sex to work together closely in a non-dating relationship, and the benefits are many.

The experience of working with a co-leader can also become one of the most serious obstacles in the program. For some peer leaders, a co-leader's differences can quickly get in the way of building a bond. Even those co-leaders who initially feel comfortable together may soon discover that their expectations will not all be met, thus creating a certain degree of tension.

It is inevitable that in any close relationship there will occasionally be misunderstanding, disappointment, competition, jealousy, and anger. It's important to identify problems when they arise and to get beyond them without threatening the co-leader bond. Better yet, co-leaders can take steps to enhance the trust and respect between them which can prevent misunderstandings from erupting.

Co-leaders can decide on the best way to approach each other before a problem occurs. It's useful to know what irritates co-leaders, to share expectations (hopes and fears) about the relationship, and to anticipate the kinds of problems which create barriers.

When there is a conflict between co-leaders, it's important to speak directly about the problem. If a peer leader is tempted to complain to others about a co-leader's incompetence or strange habits, then it's time for a face-to-face discussion before "talking behind your back" gets started. Co-leaders can set aside a regular time to meet and talk each week so that it will not be as difficult to find the time for this exchange when a conflict is apparent.

It's also important, when discussing a problem, to identify each co-leader's role in the problem and to share responsibility for making the working relationship a better one. This includes learning how to give constructive criticism tactfully and how to receive it without getting defensive.

For example, "you're lazy and can't be counted on to do your share of the work" is not as effective as "I've been on overload lately, and it would help me if we could redivide the responsibilities for our freshmen group."

After listening to a co-leader's concerns, it would certainly be more useful to respond, "Thanks for letting me know what's on your mind; let's try to work something out," rather than "I don't know what you're talking about; I do more than my share of the work as it is."

Working through conflict takes practice, patience, and a willingness on both sides to be honest and thoughtful. Learning how to be clear and direct when communicating is not easy, but there are many opportunities within the PGC program for this to happen.

In their training class, peer leaders examine their values and attitudes on a variety of topics, including peer relationships, boy-girl intimacy, drug and alcohol use, academic pressures, and conflicts with parents and other adults. They discuss common problems of adolescence and explore options for solving them. They develop skits to illustrate both the problems and alternative solutions. As part of learning how to lead discussions, they practice stating objectives, asking open-ended questions, encouraging active participation by all members of the group, thinking through problems and exploring alternatives.

A second two-day midwinter retreat reinforces and extends their skills and gives them the opportunity to share successes and concerns. They become better observers of what is happening in groups, learning to analyze the roles being played, the nature of interactions among group members, and the messages being conveyed by body language. They discuss issues of authority, hidden agendas, and conflict, and practice ways to deal with them. They also re-examine their own performance as peer leaders, emphasizing the effect of the program on their attitudes, behavior, and hopes for the future, and defining the ways in which they need to change.

Peer leaders and their faculty advisors also participate in an exciting annual event sponsored by the Princeton Center: the Urban-Suburban Peer Group Connection Conference. This event brings together 600 to 800 students and educators for a day of workshops, skits, and conversations organized around a theme such as "A Celebration of Diversity." The students are assigned to small groups that do not include anyone else from their own school, and they spend much of their time at the conference interacting with this new group. Their enthusiasm is contagious, and they leave with new friends, renewed energy, and new ideas for working with their own groups of ninth graders back home.

PROGRAM FOR FIRST YEAR STUDENTS

The program for first year students begins in late September with an all-day retreat led by peer leaders and supervised by faculty. Then, once each week from September until May, PGC co-leaders meet with groups of 10 to 15 younger students for a 45-50 minute class period during regular school hours. Faculty coordinators and advisors observe the sessions, giving feedback to the peer leaders. The learning objectives for students are:

1. To identify and appreciate the roles and responsibilities they have at school, at home, and with their friends;
2. To examine values and understand how values affect relationships with other people;
3. To become aware of and sensitive to the problems experienced by young people today, and to learn how to find solutions that promote healthy emotional, physical, and social development;
4. To improve communication skills, including the ability to express themselves clearly and to listen attentively;
5. To become more accepting of others and more respectful of differences;
6. And–extremely important to young people–to increase their self-confidence and sense of self-worth.

An important aspect of the PGC program includes reaching out to parents and encouraging their increased involvement in the school-related activities of their children. The program sponsors a Family Night attended by faculty, peer leaders, first year students, and their parents. This event has proven to be a high point for participants and has been so successful that it prompted the Princeton Center to expand its training programs to include a special series of conferences and workshops for parents, formalized as the Parent Involvement Corps. At the PGC Family Night, parents, extended family members, and even neighbors get a taste of the training in communications and group dynamics that educators and students have been given, and invariably ask for more. Perhaps the most popular activity is the "Fishbowl," where parents sit silently in a circle around a group of students who discuss questions raised by parents; then the groups trade places and parents talk about their concerns and their dreams for their children, while the students listen. Both groups come away from this exercise with new respect for each other, a better understanding of what motivates parents and young people to behave as they do, and with increased resolve to spend more time together talking about their lives and sharing their hopes for the future.

Teenagers' need for social bonding is, of course, fundamental, especially in large, often impersonal high schools where feelings of anonymity can overwhelm young people. This concern is addressed in a series of PGC activities that are a regular part of the weekly class sessions. For example, a valuable peer group activity looks at "Who has it harder in life: men or women?" Students explore the pressures and problems of being male and female from birth to old age in a debate-style format; however, there is an interesting twist. When students who support one side of the argument hear a member from the opposing side make a convincing statement, then they are obligated to switch positions. Thus, students are frequently changing sides and learn the value of an open mind, an appreciation of different points of view, and the importance of active listening.

This activity can also be an important learning experience for parents who, when discussing a controversial subject, learn to become less dogmatic and practice patience and tolerance for differences.

Evening social events are also an important component of the PGC experience. Students organize Peer Group Cabarets, olympiad activities, and beach parties–held indoors in the dead of winter–to help them become more comfortable socially, to learn how to get along across typical clique boundaries, and to develop an esprit de corps.

Finally, at the end of the year, the senior leaders and their younger peers plan a special closure experience. They examine individual and group changes, share what they have learned and how they can use the experience in other situations, and help each other through that last stage of a group's existence–Mourning/Morning–when they say goodbye to the past and welcome the future.

PROGRAM EVALUATION

According to one researcher who completed a year-long study of the program in eleven public and private schools in Atlanta, Georgia, the Peer Group Connection can help schools change in positive, constructive ways as well as help young people cope with the personal changes and challenges in their lives (Gaines, 1990). The program has been subjected to continual internal and external evaluations, and the results for schools, for educators, and for students are encouraging. According to an evaluation by the Educational Testing Service in Princeton, New Jersey, schools that establish PGC can expect a significant reduction in the number and severity of disciplinary incidents, and they can anticipate an improvement in attendance and in academic performance (Hannaway & Senior, 1989).

Teachers who serve as PGC coordinators and advisors also benefit from the program. Their evaluations of the training they receive indicate that they have developed the skills needed to reach out to today's teenagers. They welcome the opportunity to build professional relationships, ending their isolation from their colleagues and mitigating their feelings of frustration. The energy and enthusiasm that they carry away from training conferences conducted by the Princeton Center markedly reduces "teacher burnout"; in fact, many teachers who seriously considered leaving the profession find that, by working with each other and especially with their students in new ways, their enjoyment of teaching increases. They also learn how to incorporate cooperative learning experiences into their academic classes, regardless of the subject that they teach. Principals report that these teachers become more vocal at faculty meetings–often taking on new initiatives with a renewed sense of commitment and drive.

Although PGC is especially valuable for working with disaffected and high-risk teenagers, who can be found in every high school in the country, its effectiveness is by no means limited to those groups. On the contrary, it is a primary prevention model that works for *all* adolescents, including those who are or seem to be well-adjusted, helping them develop important social and coping skills.

By encouraging students to establish healthy relationships across the barriers of race, culture, socio-economic background, and age, PGC can have a positive effect on the social climate of a school. Both the first year students and seniors set ambitious goals for themselves and expect more from each other, thus encouraging more socially responsive behavior in and outside of school.

Finally, one of the most important outcomes of the PGC program derives from its modular, replicable design. It is not only the three members of the faculty team, nor the dozen or so seniors, nor even the hundred or more incoming students who benefit from PGC in any single year. By acting in ways that support everyone's efforts to grow, their example inspires others to behave in a like manner. Equally significant, however, is the fact that they have been trained to pass along to others what they have learned at PGC conferences, retreats, and classes. Moreover, the entire system in which faculty, seniors, and first year students function as teams can be multiplied as necessary throughout a school simply by increasing the number of modules.

Faculty who have experienced two years of training with the Princeton Center are able to run the PGC program in their schools, independently of the Center and with complete autonomy. In fact, over 100 high schools that have started PGC over the past thirteen years have continued the program and, in most cases, expanded it. While initial funds to implement this program may come from a combination of sources–including corporate and foundation grants–most schools pick up the ongoing costs to run this program once PGC becomes established. The exceptions include districts that have an outside corporate sponsor making a long-term commitment to this primary prevention model.

REFERENCES

Bion, W.R. (1961). *Experiences in groups and other papers.* New York: Basic Books.

Dryfoos, J.G. *(1990). Adolescents at risk: Prevalence and prevention.* New York: Oxford University Press.

Feldman, S., & Elliott, G.R. *(1990). At the threshold: The developing adolescent.* Massachusetts: Harvard University Press.

Gaines, B.D. *(1990). The Atlanta peer group connection: A qualitative evaluation of the first year's activities.*

Gardner, J.W. *(1990). On leadership.* New York: The Free Press.

Hamburg, B., & Varenhorst, B. (1972). Peer counseling in the secondary schools: Community mental health project for youth. *American Journal of Orthopsychiatry, 42*, 566-581.

Hannaway, J., & Senior, A.M. (1989). *An evaluation of the peer leadership training program: An examination of students' attitudes, behavior and performance.* Princeton, NJ: Educational Testing Services.

Mechem, E. (1943). Affectivity and growth in children. *Child Development, 14*, 90-115.

Powell, S.R. *(1988). The peer group handbook.* Lawrenceville, NJ: Princeton Center for Leadership Training.

Silber, E. et al. (1961). Adaptive behavior in competent adolescents. *Archives of General Psychiatry, 5*, 354-365.

Stanford, G. *(1977). Developing effective classroom groups: A practical guide for teachers.* New York: Hart Publishing Company.

Theobald, R. *(1987). The rapids of change: Social entrepreneurship in turbulent times.* Bloomington, IN: Knowledge Systems.

Social Skills Intervention Guide: Systematic Approaches to Social Skills Training

Frank M. Gresham
University of California

Stephen N. Elliott
University of Wisconsin-Madison

SUMMARY. Social skills training procedures that can be used in a group format are described. These procedures are contained in the *Social Skills Intervention Guide* (Elliott & Gresham, 1991) which is a systematic approach to teaching social skills to children between the ages of 6 and 16 years. A system for classifying social skills deficits based on acquisition/performance deficits and presence/absence of interfering problem behaviors is described. Implementation issues such as selection and grouping of students, establishing group rules, and monitoring progress are also described as well as a means of monitoring student progress in social skills training groups.

The ability to interact successfully with one's peers and significant adults is arguably one of the most important aspects of a child's

---

Address correspondence to: Dr. Frank M. Gresham, School of Education, University of California, Riverside, CA 92521.

[Haworth co-indexing entry note]: "Social Skills Intervention Guide: Systematic Approaches to Social Skills Training." Gresham, Frank M., and Stephen N. Elliott. Co-published simultaneously in *Special Services in the Schools* (The Haworth Press, Inc.) Vol. 8, No. 1, 1993, pp. 137-158; and: *Promoting Student Success Through Group Interventions* (ed: Joseph E. Zins, and Maurice J. Elias) The Haworth Press, Inc., 1993, pp. 137-158. Multiple copies of this article/chapter may be purchased from The Haworth Document Delivery Center [1-800-3-HAWORTH; 9:00 a.m. - 5:00 p.m. (EST)].

development. All major developmental theorists (e.g., Erikson, 1963; Kohlberg, 1969; Piaget, 1952) delineated stages of social and moral development during which social competence evolves. Social skills represent the tools children use to establish and maintain positive relationships with peers and adults.

Social skills in school settings are important for several reasons. Children who experience peer relationship difficulties have a high incidence of school maladjustment, school suspensions/expulsions, dropping out of school, delinquency, childhood psychopathology, and adult mental health difficulties (Asher & Hymel, 1981; Gresham, 1981a, 1981b; Hartup, 1983; Parker & Asher, 1987; Roff, Sells, & Golden, 1972).

Further, peer relationship difficulties have been shown to differentiate children with mild disabilities (e.g., learning disabilities, behavior disorders, and mild mental retardation) from their nondisabled peers (Bryan, 1976, 1978; Gottlieb, 1981; Gottlieb & Leyser, 1981; Gresham, 1982, 1988; Walker & McConnell, 1988). In addition, children with mild disabilities who are educated in regular classrooms are more often poorly accepted, neglected, or socially rejected by their nondisabled peers (Gresham, 1982).

Finally, social skills have been related to other indices of classroom functioning, particularly academic achievement and so-called "academic survival skills" (Cartledge & Milburn, 1983; Gresham & Elliott, 1990; Gresham & Reschly, 1988; Hops & Walker, 1976; Walker & McConnell, 1988). In many cases, the probability that children will be referred to special education depends in large part on their level of academic-related social skills functioning (e.g., paying attention, completing work, ignoring peer distractions, etc.) in the regular classroom (Gresham & Elliott, 1990; Hersh & Walker, 1983; Stephens, 1978; Walker & McConnell, 1988).

Clearly, children with social skills deficits are likely to experience a number of negative outcomes ranging from peer relationship difficulties to long-term psychological adjustment problems in adulthood. The purpose of the present article is to provide a description of procedures that can be used in a group format to intervene with children's social skills deficits. We will present definitions of social skills and social competence followed by a description of the *Social Skills Intervention Guide* (SSIG) (Elliott & Gresham, 1991) which is a comprehensive social skills training program for children between the ages of 6 and 16 years. Various implementation issues such as selection, grouping, formation of group rules, and monitoring student progress are discussed.

DEFINITION AND CLASSIFICATION ISSUES

Definition

Social skill is a term that is used frequently, but often has various connotations for different people. Some individuals may define a person as socially skilled if that person is well-accepted by peers. Others may define social skills as behaviors that result in reciprocal positive social exchanges among two or more persons. On a general level, social skills might be defined as socially acceptable behaviors that enable a person to interact effectively with others and to avoid socially unacceptable responses from others (Gresham & Elliott, 1990).

Gresham (1983) proposed a *social validity* definition of social skills which represents a useful and objective definition. According to this definition:

> Social skills are those behaviors that occur in specific situations which predict important social outcomes for children and youth.

In most settings relevant for children, important social outcomes may include: (a) peer acceptance, (b) significant others' judgments of social skill, (c) academic achievement, (d) positive feelings of self-worth, and (e) positive adaptation to school, home, and community environments.

Social skills represent behaviors in specific situations which result in judgments of social competence (McFall, 1982). Thus, social skills are specific behaviors which lead others to judge whether or not a behavioral performance was competent. Judgments by others play a significant role in social skills because, ultimately, all social behavior occurs in contexts in which others are making judgments regarding the appropriateness or inappropriateness of behavior.

The social validity definition has the advantage of specifying behaviors in which a child is deficient, but also can define these behaviors as socially skilled based on their relationship to socially important outcomes. Social validity represents an important type of validity in interventions with children. Social validity refers to establishing the *social significance* of the goals of intervention, using intervention procedures that are *socially acceptable* to treatment consumers, and producing *socially important* effects with those interventions (Kazdin, 1977; Wolf, 1978).

Classification of Social Skills Deficits

Most authors agree that social incompetencies observed in children result from difficulties in either the *acquisition* or *performance* of social behaviors (Bandura, 1977). Kratochwill and French (1984) suggested that response acquisition (skill deficits) "occur when the individual has not learned skills that are necessary to exhibit a socially competent response whereas performance deficits arise when the child fails to successfully perform behaviors he or she is capable of" (p. 332).

Gresham and Elliott (1990) extended this two-way classification scheme to include four general areas of social skills difficulties. This scheme incorporates two dimensions of behavior: (a) social skills and (b) interfering problem behaviors. Children may have acquisition or performance deficits with or without interfering problem behaviors. Interfering problem behaviors (e.g., anxiety, aggression, impulsivity, etc.) may prevent either the acquisition or performance of socially skilled behavior.

Classification of social skills deficits in this manner is important because it identifies the type of social skill deficit (acquisition or performance) and specifies interfering problem behaviors that must be part of the focus of intervention. Acquisition and performance deficits dictate differential intervention strategies which are discussed later in this article.

PHILOSOPHICAL BASIS OF SOCIAL SKILLS TRAINING

A fundamental assumption upon which social skills training rests is that children learn social skills through the process of observational learning, instrumental (operant) learning, and respondent (classical) learning (Elliott & Gresham, 1991). Numerous variables may account for children's deficits in prosocial behavior: however, many of these variables are either inferred (e.g., poor ego controls, repressed hostile feelings, etc.) or are beyond anyone's control (e.g., developmental immaturity, inadequate cognitive abilities, etc.).

Based on the work of Michelson, Sugai, Wood, and Kazdin (1983), we make five fundamental assumptions regarding our conceptualization of social skills:

Assumption 1: Social skills are primarily acquired through learning that involves observation, modeling, rehearsal, and feedback.

Assumption 2: Social skills include specific, discrete verbal and nonverbal behaviors.

Assumption 3: Social skills require both effective and appropriate initiations of behavior and responses to the behavior of others.

Assumption 4: Social skills are interactive by nature and entail effective and appropriate behavioral performances.

Assumption 5: Social skills are situationally-specific behaviors and are influenced by the characteristics, demands, and expectations operating in specific environments.

Gresham and Elliott (1991) have described a model of variables that influence children's social skills deficits and which can be used to remediate social skill deficiencies. In this model, social skills deficits may result from five factors: (a) a lack of cues or opportunities to learn or perform prosocial behaviors, (b) the presence of interfering problem behaviors that either block acquisition or impede performance of prosocial behaviors, (c) a lack of knowledge, (d) a lack of sufficient practice or feedback on prosocial behavioral performances, and (e) a lack of reinforcement for performance of socially skilled behaviors. Deficient social skills for a particular child may result from one or a combination of these five factors.

Social Skills Training Variables

Four fundamental processes underlie all social skills training techniques discussed in this article and form the basis of the SSIG (Elliott & Gresham, 1991). These training variables are: instruction, rehearsal, feedback/reinforcement, and reductive procedures and they are based in part on the theoretical work of Ladd and Mize (1983). Each of these variables is discussed briefly in the following sections.

Instruction. There are fundamentally two types of instruction: verbal and modeled. Verbal instruction typically involves the use of spoken language to describe, prompt, explain, define, or request social behavior. Verbal instruction may involve the use of concrete or abstract concepts to facilitate the acquisition of social skills. The training procedures of coaching and direct instruction rely, in large part, on verbal instruction.

Modeled instruction involves the use of live or filmed (videotaped) performances or enactments of social skills. The major advantage of modeled instruction is that children learn how to combine, chain, and sequence behaviors that comprise a particular social skill. The adage, "a picture is worth a thousand words" captures the essence of modeled instruction.

Rehearsal. Rehearsal is the repeated practice of a social skill that promotes retention of the skill concept and more effective behavioral performance. Rehearsal can be *overt, covert*, or *verbal.* Overt rehearsal, typically called behavioral rehearsal, involves the repeated practice of external behaviors involved in the performance of a social skill. Covert rehearsal of instructed social skills allows not only for retention of instructed information, but also for more effective overt performances of the social skill. Verbal rehearsal entails the verbal report or recitation of the components of a particular social skill.

In short, verbal rehearsal involves the learner stating what he or she might do in a particular social situation; covert rehearsal involves the learner thinking, imagining, or self-talking rather than verbalizing or actually performing a social skill; overt rehearsal involves the learner actually performing the social skill.

Feedback/reinforcement. Feedback refers to information provided to the learner regarding the correspondence between a social skill performance and a standard of performance. Feedback can take two forms: evaluative and informative. Evaluative feedback informs the learner of the extent to which a given behavioral performance matched an external criterion or standard of performance. Informative feedback gives the learner specific information regarding the reasons for correct or incorrect performances of a given social skill. Informative feedback is the preferred type of feedback to be used in social skills training because it allows for modification of behavioral performances.

Reinforcement involves the presentation or removal of environmental events that increase the frequency of behavior. Reinforcement can be either positive or negative. With positive reinforcement, an environmental event is *presented* which increases the frequency of a behavior. Positive reinforcement is used frequently in social skills training groups in the form of praise, access to preferred activities, attendance stars, and the like.

With negative reinforcement, an environmental event is *removed* that increases the frequency of behavior. Negative reinforcement always involves either escape or avoidance learning. That is, an individual's behavior will be negatively reinforced if that behavior allows the person to escape or avoid an aversive stimulus. For example, some children in classrooms exhibit disruptive behavior in order to avoid academic assignments which they consider aversive. Negative reinforcement is not used as frequently in the context of social skills training groups as positive reinforcement.

Reductive processes. Social skills training, by definition, focuses on teaching prosocial behaviors to students. However, the presence of interfering problem behaviors will often hinder the effective teaching of social skills as well as effective classroom learning.

Reductive procedures present or remove environmental events with the goal of problem behavior to occur less frequently. These procedures, to be discussed later, include response cost, timeout, overcorrection, and differential reinforcement techniques.

SOCIAL SKILLS TRAINING OBJECTIVES

As a treatment process, social skills training has four objectives: (a) promoting the acquisition of social skills, (b) enhancing the performance of social skills, (c) removing interfering problem behaviors, and (d) facilitating generalization of socially skilled behavior. These objectives reflect the type of social skill deficiency (i.e., acquisition versus performance deficits), the presence or absence of interfering problem behaviors, and the functional control of social behaviors in specific situations.

In social skills training one needs to recognize that a given child may have some acquisition deficits, some performance deficits, and some interfering problem behaviors. As such, group leaders must match the appropriate training strategy with the appropriate deficit or behavioral excess the child possesses. Additionally, a common misconception is that one seeks to facilitate generalization *after* presenting procedures for acquisition or performance as part of some final stage of treatment. The evidence is clear that best practice is to incorporate generalization from the very beginning of any social skills training program. In this way, students are better prepared to demonstrate learned behaviors in other settings and situations.

Promoting Skill Acquisition

Procedures classified under this category represent major ways in which the *acquisition* of social skills can be facilitated. These procedures include when students do not have a particular social skill in their repertoire or when they do not know a particular step in the performance of a behavioral sequence. These strategies should be employed after classifying students' social skills problems as acquisition deficits.

Three procedures represent the pathways to remediation of social skill acquisition deficits. In addition, social problem solving represent another pathway, but is not discussed here due to space limitations and the fact that it incorporates the three procedures to be discussed in this section.

Modeling or observational learning is the process of learning a behavior by observing another individual perform that behavior. Modeling instruction presents the entire sequence of behaviors involved in a particular social skill and teaches how to integrate specific behaviors in this sequence into a composite behavioral pattern. Modeling represents one of the most effective and efficient ways of teaching social behavior. (Bandura, 1977; Gresham, 1985).

Coaching refers to the use of verbal instruction to teach social skills. Unlike modeling, which emphasizes visual displays of a social skill, coaching emphasizes a child's cognitive and language skills. Coaching involves three fundamental steps: (a) presenting social concepts or rules, (b) providing opportunities for practice or rehearsal of a social skill, and (c) providing specific informational feedback on a behavioral performance.

With coaching, one can transmit general principles of social interaction, integrate behavioral sequences in performing a social skill, set social goals of an interaction sequence, and help students become aware of their social impact on others (Renshaw & Asher, 1983). The assumption is that children can use general principles of social interaction to guide their behavior in specific social situations. In this sense, coaching is based, in part, on the notion of "rule-governed" rather than "contingency-shaped" behavior. In a rule-governed approach, one does not have to teach each and every situation a child is likely to encounter. Rather, the goal is to teach social rules that a child can apply to a variety of situations.

Behavioral rehearsal refers to practicing a newly learned behavior in the structured, protective situation of role playing. Through this process, students enhance their proficiency in using the skill without experiencing adverse consequences. Social learning theory suggests that behavioral rehearsal is essential to learning social behavior (Bandura, 1977).

There are three forms of behavioral rehearsal which can be used in a number of ways and combinations. For example, one could ask students to imagine a social situation in which another child is teasing them and then to imagine how they would respond (covert rehearsal). Next, one might combine covert rehearsal with verbal rehearsal by asking students to recite the specific behaviors they would exhibit in imagined situations. Finally, one might combine covert and verbal with overt rehearsal by asking students to role-play the imagined situation.

Enhancing Skill Performance

As previously discussed, many social skills deficits represent *performance* (won't do) rather than acquisition (can't do) deficits. That is, failure to perform certain social skills in specific situations may be due to inappropriately arranged antecedents or a lack of appropriate consequences for the performance of prosocial behaviors. A number of specific procedures can be classified under the broad rubrics of antecedent and consequent strategies.

Antecedent strategies. Two general strategies fall under the category of antecedent strategies: peer initiation and cuing/prompting. With peer initiation strategies, a child's peers are used to initiate and maintain social interactions with socially isolated or withdrawn students. These strategies are most effective with students with performance deficits and who evidence relatively low rates of social interaction.

In using peer initiation strategies, peer confederates are recruited and instructed in the specific behaviors required to initiate and maintain a social interaction. Specific feedback is given to peer confederates based on role-played examples of peer initiation. Finally, peer confederates are instructed to initiate interactions with targeted children and to report any problems they may have had in their initiation efforts. Peer initiations are an excellent strategy to use in social skills training groups containing socially withdrawn or shy students.

Cuing and prompting makes use of verbal or nonverbal cues or prompts for a child to engage in prosocial behaviors. For example, in some cases, a simple prompt or cue may be all children need to initiate a social interaction. However, total reliance on this procedure, particularly with severely withdrawn students, has a relatively small chance of producing permanent changes in social behavior.

Consequent strategies. Intervention strategies relying on consequent control techniques can be classified into three categories: (a) reinforcement-based strategies, (b) behavioral contracts, and (c) school-home notes. Reinforcement-based strategies rely on the presentation or removal of events that occur as a result of a given social behavior. Reinforcement-based strategies assume that the child knows how to perform a behavior, but is not doing so because he or she is not given reinforcement to increase the frequency of a behavior and to improve the quality of a social skill performance.

One frequently used reinforcement strategy involves praising a child and providing other positive attention when the child displays appropriate social behavior. Other types of positive reinforcers such as tokens, points, star charts, access to preferred activities, and the like are examples of positive reinforcement techniques.

Another reinforcement-based strategy that is relevant to small groups is the *interdependent group-oriented contingency.* With this system, the same behaviors are expected for all group members and reinforcement for the group is based on the performance of the group as a whole. This strategy is effective in motivating group members to participate in group exercises and in reducing inappropriate behavior in the group. An easy way to do this in a group is to divide the group time into five-to-ten minute intervals and award a point to the group if within this time span every student meets an explicitly set criterion for participation and/or compliance with group rules. If the group earns 80-90 percent of the total number of possible points, the group is awarded a preferred reinforcer. These contingencies can be applied for each group session as well as across sessions for an entire week. Inappropriate group behavior can be controlled by taking points away from the entire group based on misbehavior or violation of group rules.

Behavioral contracts are written agreements between you and students that specify the relationship between behavior and its consequences. Behavioral contracts have the following five components: (a) specification of mutual gains between you and the student, (b) the ways in which the student will demonstrate the behavior in an observable way, (c) a provision for sanctions for not meeting the terms of the contract, (d) a bonus clause for consistent performance of desired behaviors, and (e) a means of monitoring reinforcers given and received (Stuart, 1971).

Before starting a social skills training group, be sure to write a behavioral contract for behaviors to be performed in the group and criteria for group participation. In addition, personalized contracts written for individual students who need work on unique skills or for students who are disruptive or troublesome may be beneficial.

School-home notes are notes sent by group leaders to parents each day or week. These notes represent a frequent and formal means of communication between the school and home regarding the student's school behavior. One can easily apprise parents or guardians of the current topics or skills being covered by social skills groups. In fact, an efficient means of using school-home notes is to incorporate them into a behavioral contract. In this way, group leaders can enlist parental cooperation for the prosocial behaviors being taught in their group. School-home notes should be brief, clear, and include only those behaviors that are objective and observable.

Removing Interfering Problem Behaviors

Clearly, social skills training focuses on the facilitation of prosocial behaviors. However, the social skills classification model presented earlier distinguishes between acquisition and performance deficits that are associated with interfering problem behaviors. Students may either fail to acquire or fail to perform certain social skills because problem behaviors interfere with or block their acquisition or performance of a social skill.

Three general strategies may be used to remove or reduce interfering problem behaviors: (a) differential reinforcement, (b) positive practice, and (c) response cost. In differential reinforcement, behavior is reinforced in the presence of one stimulus and that same behavior is not reinforced in the presence of another stimulus. That is, the purpose of differential reinforcement is to get a behavior under stimulus control.

One differential reinforcement technique is known as *differential reinforcement of other behavior* (DRO). DRO refers to the delivery of a reinforcer after any appropriate behavior except the target behavior selected for reduction. The effect of DRO is to reduce a target behavior and increase other behaviors. Another differential reinforcement technique is *differential reinforcement of low rates of behavior* (DRL). In DRL, a specific number of reductions in a target behavior in a specified time interval is reinforced. For example, DRL can be used in groups by setting a criterion of occurrences of misbehavior (e.g., three or fewer in 45 minutes) and reinforcing the group if they have three or fewer instances of the misbehavior. A final differential reinforcement strategy is *differential reinforcement of incompatible behavior* (DRI). In DRI, behaviors are reinforced that are incompatible with the targeted problem behavior. For example, talking nicely to others is incompatible with cursing others. Thus, if talking nicely is reinforced more frequently than cursing, then talking nicely will increase in frequency and cursing will decrease in frequency.

Positive practice is a component of overcorrection that reduces the frequency of problem behavior. It refers to the repeated practice of an appropriate behavior that is incompatible with an inappropriate behavior. For example, if a student insulted another student (e.g., "You're really stupid"), he or she would have to practice saying nice things or giving compliments to the insulted child, to each person in the group, and even the group leader.

Because positive practice serves an educational function by teaching the appropriate behavioral alternative to an inappropriate behavior, this component of overcorrection is relevant to social skills training. Positive practice should be part of every social skills training group because group leaders can use behavioral incidents which occur in group as a basis for positive practice of social skills.

Response cost refers to removing a specified amount of a positive reinforcer to decrease the frequency of a targeted behavior. In practice, response cost usually takes the form of fines or penalties for inappropriate behavior. Response cost can be easily applied in the context of a social skills training group. For example, a set number of points can be awarded to the group and/or individual students before each group session and points can be removed each time students violate group rules. Response cost can be used in conjunction with group contingency systems, school-home note systems, and behavioral contracts. The chief advantage of response cost is the ease of application relative to more labor-intensive reductive procedures such as DRO, DRL, and DRI.

Facilitating Generalization

The ultimate goal of social skills training in groups is to have trained behaviors occur in other settings, situations, and to be maintained over time. Generalization can be thought of in terms of three parameters: (a) setting generalization, (b) behavior generalization, and (c) time generalization.

Setting generalization refers to the occurrence of a behavior in settings or situations other than those in which social skills training takes place. The reason behavior generalizes across settings or situations is that settings and situations often share common properties. The more closely the training group setting parallels settings beyond it, the greater the potential degree of generalization.

Behavior generalization refers to changes in behavior that are not the direct focus of one's social skills training; that is, a student performs a different behavior in the presence of the same stimulus. If behaviors are members of the same functional response class (i.e., the same antecedent and/or consequent events control the behavior), one can facilitate behavior generalization by teaching only a subset of the response class.

Time generalization refers to the continuation or maintenance of behavior in an intervention setting after an intervention program has been withdrawn. Several factors account for time generalization or maintenance of behavior. Some social behaviors taught in social skills training have a high probability of being reinforced in the future (e.g., courteous, friendly behaviors are likely to be reinforced). Some behaviors taught in social skills training produce their own reinforcing consequences (e.g., conversation skills and play skills are sometimes self-reinforcing). Finally, some behaviors taught in social skills training may produce permanent changes in the behavior of significant others such as parents or teachers. In other words, because the student has changed, others may react differently to the student.

Two general strategies are discussed as being useful in facilitating generalization: (a) training diversely and (b) teaching relevant behaviors (Stokes & Osnes, 1986). To train diversely, you need to use sufficient *stimulus exemplars* and sufficient *response exemplars*. The former deals with settings and situations and is a means of programming setting generalization; the latter deals with multiple ways of responding to the *same* situation and is a means of programming behavior generalization.

One provides diverse stimulus exemplars by using as many and varied conditions under which to teach a social skill as possible. One Provides varied sufficient response exemplars, you need to teach the student as many ways as possible to respond in the same social setting or situation (i.e., give students plenty of behavioral "ammunition"). This is especially useful, for example, when teaching learning disabled or mildly retarded students how to cope with teasing by peers on the bus or in the lunchroom.

Teaching relevant behaviors is another way to promote generalization. To get a behavior to enter an environment that reinforces the behavior without any special programming, relevant behaviors need to be taught. In this sense, social skills are relevant behaviors. However, the relevance of a particular social skill depends upon the behavioral standards, expectations, and requirements of a particular social environment. In order to teach relevant behaviors for a given environment, you need to know what is relevant in that environment.

The behaviors you teach in your social skills training group should have social validity. That is, the behaviors should be socially significant behaviors as judged by significant others in the student's environment. By teaching behaviors considered socially significant by others, you increase the chances that these behaviors will enter a natural community of reinforcement.

SOCIAL SKILLS TAUGHT IN THE SSIG

The social skills taught in the SSIG are those assessed by the *Social Skills Rating System* (SSRS)(Gresham & Elliott, 1990). The SSRS is a multirater (teacher, parent, and student), nationally standardized series of rating scales for students between the ages of 3-18 years. Specifically, these skills involve five domains of social behavior: *cooperation, assertion, responsibility, empathy, and self-control (CARES)*. For purposes of social skills training, these domains are broken down into subdomain behaviors. The domains and subdomains of the SSRS and the SSIG can be found in publications by Gresham and Elliott (1990) and Elliott and Gresham (1991).

Each domain except Responsibility has two skill subdomains. The Cooperation Domain contains the skills of classroom interaction and working and playing together. The Assertion Domain contains the skills of conversation and joining and volunteering. The Empathy Domain contains the skills of active listening and positive feedback. Finally, the Self-Control Domain contains the skills of conflict resolution and anger control.

The SSIG teaches 43 social skills in the aforementioned domains and subdomains: however, these are only a subset of the social skills students need to interact successfully in their varying environments. One may choose to expand upon the behavioral repertoires of children over the course of various skill training sessions. Similarly, group leaders will tend to personalize many of the role-play situations that the SSIG presents. The predictable training format of the SSIG readily facilitates such adaptations.

Implementation Issues in Social Skills Training

Significant challenges confront you as you select, implement, and evaluate interventions for children with social behavior problems. In most cases, the major challenge is not a scarcity of potential treatments. Instead, a need for a technology that clearly links assessment results to interventions, a way to systematically conceptualize the problem you want to treat, and a lack of teacher or parent involvement will challenge you.

With the SSRS and the SSIG, you can overcome the first two problems. In addition, you can indirectly facilitate parent and teacher involvement in the intervention process by using their observations via SSRS ratings to start your planning. Teachers and parents can also play a valuable role in the implementation of the intervention program, particularly during the Follow Through and Practice and Generalization phases. Several of these implementation issues are discussed briefly in the following sections.

Linking Assessment Results to Interventions

The basis for linking assessment results to general intervention procedures in the SSIG lies in the conceptualization of social skills deficits drawn from SSRS ratings. Specifically, by using the SSRS, you can characterize social skills problems as acquisition or performance deficits. In addition to social skills deficits, the SSRS provides you with information about social skills strengths, interfering problem behaviors, and poor academic functioning that may interfere with the production of social skills.

The combined assessment results for social skills and interfering problem behaviors provides the basis for a six-category classification scheme. Most children exhibit some social behaviors in each of the six categories. These categories include the four categories described earlier (acquisition or performance deficits with or without interfering problem behaviors) as well as social skills *strengths* with the absence or presence of interfering problem behaviors. This classification scheme is pivotal to the linking of assessment results to intervention plans.

SELECTING AND GROUPING STUDENTS

You must base your decision about student selection and group size on factors such as your own experience, the work space, and the time available for social skills training groups. You will generally find that groups of three to six children, meeting twice a week for 45 to 60 minutes is most effective.

To give more attention to the participating students and to provide a second "actor" for role playing, working with a co-leader can be helpful. This co-worker can be a socially skilled student (often in a higher grade than group members), a teacher, a parent volunteer, or another special service provider. The use of a group co-leader often increases the quality and quantity of treatment services.

Use of the SSRS as a selection instrument allows for building small groups of students with well-defined difficulties in social skills. Generally, working with students who have similar problems is advantageous because the skill units will directly apply to most of the students in the group.

However, the use of homogenous groups is not required because other students with differing problems can serve as positive models for each other. Moreover, the training provides them with opportunities to practice skills and to be reinforced for appropriate behaviors. Remember that the group itself is a social unit and provides rich opportunities for reinforcing existing social skills, refining skills, and teaching new skills.

Parental Permission and Involvement

Parent support is an important ingredient in any endeavor with children. Requirements for parental permission for a student to participate in social skills training groups vary across settings. Regardless, one should obtain parental permission as a condition for participation for all school-based groups. Asking for parental permission is more than a perfunctory legal step; it represents the opening of a significant line of communication about a student on the part of adults who want to improve the student's effectiveness in interacting with others.

Parental involvement can be encouraged by having them take part in the Follow Through and Practice and Generalization phases of social skills training. "Homework" assignments that encourage wider use and application of social skills they have learned in group can lead to generalization. As often as possible in these homework assignments, involve discussions with a parent about how and when specific social skills are used in the child's daily activities at work and play. Parent meetings at mid- and post-group also can be of much benefit.

Working with Groups of Students

Running social skills training groups requires that you have more than just good social skills and knowledge of social skills training techniques. One must understand group dynamics. Moreover, one must be "with it" in terms of current student events and communication techniques. Finally, one must provide and consistently follow ground rules for group interactions.

In terms of group dynamics, establish early the goals of group training sessions and state your leadership responsibilities. Students generally want to know what you expect of them and who will provide leadership for the group. If you do not clarify these points at the outset, the group may spend several sessions "forming," "storming," and "norming" (Tuckman & Jensen, 1977). Forming involves the development of attraction bonds and the exchange of basic information among group participants. Storming involves dissatisfaction with others in the group and often disagreement about group procedures. Norming is a stage in which a group starts to establish roles and cohesiveness. You can hasten the development of this stage by sharing rules and by expressing support and optimism.

Rules for group functioning vary with the size of the group and your own teaching and relating style. However, when establishing group rules for social skills intervention activities, consider the following common areas: (a) *attendance*, (b) *punctuality*, (c) *participation*, (d) *confidentiality*, (e) *taking turns speaking and being a good listener,* (f) *providing constructive feedback,* and (g) *homework assignments.*

During the first group session, discuss the formation of rules pertinent to the seven areas listed above. Once group rules are formulated and agreed upon, post them where the group meets. Review these rules periodically.

At the first group meeting, one must discuss the purpose of the group. To introduce this, you and the students can be helped to make straightforward statements about how social skills enhance one's relationships with people and are important in everyday life. In addition, stories or videotapes that feature the importance of cooperation, self-control, and other socially relevant behaviors can help focus students or group goals. Regardless of how one discusses the purpose of the group, inform the students that just as schools help them acquire reading, writing, and arithmetic skills, so their school wants to help them acquire and express social skills.

Monitoring Student Progress

The goal of any treatment program is change. In the case of social skills training, you can see when students increase their performance of desired social behaviors and decrease their performance of problem behaviors. Group leaders are responsible for monitoring student progress. Progress monitoring should involve a combination of the following techniques: pre-treatment and post-treatment SSRS ratings, direct observations during role-play sessions, and brief periodic interviews with students' teachers and parents.

Sample progress monitoring forms can be found in the SSIG (Elliott & Gresham, 1991) and can be used by group leaders to determine mastery levels of social skills. These forms are a useful vehicle for feedback to both students, group leaders, and parents depicting progress made in social skills training groups.

CONCLUSION

Social skills represent vitally important behaviors for children and youth. The degree to which students interact positively with peers and adults predicts both short-term and long-term adjustment. In addition, social skills functioning is related to academic success, peer acceptance, and positive mental health functioning.

Some children experience difficulty in either acquiring or performing prosocial behaviors. This is especially true of children with mild disabilities (e.g., learning disabled, behaviorally disordered, mildly mentally retarded). There is also a sizeable percentage of nondisabled children who experience difficulties in peer relationships.

We believe that social skills training in a group format described in this article holds promise for remediating deficits in prosocial behavior. The strategies discussed in this article have been shown to be among the most effective techniques for teaching social skills to children and youth (Elliott & Gresham, 1991; Gresham, 1985; Schneider & Bryne, 1985). Using a systematic means of selecting social skills for intervention (e.g., the SSRS), employing proven social skills intervention techniques (e.g., modeling, coaching, reinforcement-based procedures, etc.), and attending to generalization techniques (e.g., training diversely and teaching relevant behaviors) will facilitate the acquisition of socially significant behaviors that predict important social outcomes for children and youth.

REFERENCES

Asher, S., & Hymel, S. (1981). Children's social competence in peer relations: Sociometric and behavioral assessment. In J. Wine & M. Smye (Eds.), *Social competence* (pp. 125-157). New York: Guilford Press.

Bandura, A. (1977). *Social learning theory*. Englewood Cliffs, NJ: Prentice-Hall.

Bryan, T. (1976). Peer popularity of learning disabled children: A replication. *Journal of Learning Disabilities, 9*, 307-311.

Bryan, T. (1978). Social relationships and verbal interactions of learning disabled children. *Journal of Learning Disabilities, 11*, 107-115.

Cartledge, G., & Milburn, J. (1983). Social skill assessment and teaching in the schools. In T. Kratochwill (Ed.), *Advances in school psychology* (pp. 175-236). Hillsdale, NJ: Lawrence Erlbaum.

Elliott, S.N., & Gresham, F.M. (1991). *Social skills intervention guide: Practical strategies for social skills training*. Circle Pines, MN: American Guidance Service.

Erikson, E. (1963). *Childhood and society*. New York: Norton.

Gottlieb, J. (1981). Mainstreaming: Fulfilling the promise. *American Journal of Mental Deficiency, 86*, 115-126.

Gottlieb, J., & Leyser, Y. (1981). Facilitating the social mainstreaming of retarded children. *Exceptional Education Quarterly, 1*, 57-70.

Gresham, F.M. (1981a). Assessment of children's social skills. *Journal of School Psychology, 19*, 120-133.

Gresham, F.M. (1981b). Social skills training with handicapped children: A review. *Review of Educational Research, 51*, 139-176.

Gresham, F.M. (1982). Misguided mainstreaming: The case for social skills training with handicapped children. *Exceptional Children, 48*, 420-433.

Gresham, F.M. (1985). Utility of cognitive-behavioral procedures for social skills training with children. *Journal of Abnormal Child Psychology, 13*, 411-423.

Gresham, F.M. (1988). Social skills: Conceptual and applied aspects of assessment, training, and social validation. In J. Witt, S. Elliott, & F. Gresham (Eds.), *Handbook of behavior therapy in education* (pp. 523-546). New York: Plenum Press.

Gresham, F.M., & Elliott, S.N. (1990). *Social Skills Rating System*. Circle Pines, MN: American Guidance Service.

Gresham, F.M., & Reschly, D.J. (1988). Issues in the conceptualization, classification, and assessment of social skills in the mildly handicapped. In T. Kratochwill (Ed.), *Advances in school psychology* (pp. 203-247). Hillsdale, NJ: Lawrence Erlbaum.

Hartup, W. (1983). Peer relations. In P. Mussen (Series Ed.), & E. Heterington (Vol. Ed.), *Handbook of child psychology, Vol. 4: Socialization, personality. and social development* (pp. 103-196). New York: Wiley.

Hersh, R., & Walker, H. (1983). Great expectations: Making schools effective for all students. *Policy Studies Review, 2*, 147-188.

Kazdin, A. (1977). Assessing the clinical or applied importance of behavior change through social validation. *Behavior Modification, 1*, 427-451.

Kohlberg, L. (1969). Stage and sequence: The cognitive-developmental approach to socialization. In D. Goslin (Ed.), *Handbook of socialization theory and research*. Chicago: Rand McNally.

Kratochwill, T., & French, D. (1984). Social skills training with withdrawn children. *School Psychology Review, 13*, 331-338.

Ladd, G., & Mize, J. (1983). A cognitive-social learning model of social skill training. *Psychological Review, 90*, 127-157.

Michelson, L., Sugai, D., Wood, R., & Kazdin, A. (1983). *Social skills assessment and training with children: An empirically based approach*. New York: Plenum Press.

Parker, J., & Asher, S. (1987). Peer relations and later personal adjustment: Are low-accepted children at risk? *Psychological Bulletin, 102*, 357-389.

Piaget, J. (1952). *The moral judgment of the child*. New York: Collier.

Renshaw, P., & Asher, S. (1983). Children's goals and strategies for social interaction. *Merrill-Palmer Quarterly, 29*, 353-374.

Roff, M., Sells, B., & Golden, M. (1972). *Social adjustment and personality adjustment in children*. Minneapolis, MN: University of Minnesota Press.

Schneider, B., & Bryne, B. (1985). Children's social skills training: A meta-analysis. In B. Schneider, K. Rubin, & J. Ledingham (Eds.), *Children's peer relations: Issues in assessment and intervention* (pp. 175-190). New York: Springer-Verlag.

Stephens, T. (1978). *Social skills in the classroom*. Columbus, OH: Cedars Press.

Stokes, T., & Osnes, P. (1986). Programming the generalization of children's social behavior. In P. Strain, M. Guralnick, & H. Walker (Eds.), *Children's social behavior: Development, assessment and modification* (pp. 407-443). Orlando, FL: Academic Press.

Stuart, R. (1971). Behavioral contracting with families of delinquents. *Journal of Behavior Therapy and Experimental Psychiatry, 2*, 1-11.

Tuckman, B., & Jensen, M. (1977). Stages of small group development revisited. *Group and Organization, 2*, 419-427.

Walker, H., & McConnell, S. (1988). *Walker-McConnell Scale of social Competence and School Adjustment*. Austin, TX: PRO-ED.

Wolf, M. (1978). Social validity: The case for subjective measurement or how applied behavior analysis is finding its heart. *Journal of Applied Behavior Analysis, 11*, 203-214.

Stabilizing Classroom-Based Group Interventions: Guidelines for Special Services Providers and Consultants

Bonnie A. Robinson
Maurice J. Elias

Rutgers University

SUMMARY. Group interventions are an important aspect of the roles of professionals in the schools. The literature on school based group interventions primarily provides a description of specific interventions and their component parts, with instructional steps for implementation. However, for a school based group intervention to be successful, the intervention must become institutionalized in the system within which it is being implemented, and planning for institutionalization must begin at the earliest stages of program or intervention design. This article provides guidelines for the professional working in the schools to follow to facilitate the long-term stabilization or institutionalization of an intervention. Structures that consultants and/or implementers can establish to help operationalize the guidelines are described and illustrated through case examples with em-

---

Address correspondence to: Dr. Maurice J. Elias, Department of Psychology, Rutgers University, Livingston Campus, New Brunswick, NJ 08903.

[Haworth co-indexing entry note]: "Stabilizing Classroom-Based Group Interventions: Guidelines for Special Services Providers and Consultants." Robinson, Bonnie A., and Maurice J. Elias. Co-published simultaneously in *Special Services in the Schools* (The Haworth Press, Inc.) Vol. 8, No. 1, 1993, pp. 159-177; and: *Promoting Student Success Through Group Interventions* (ed: Joseph E. Zins, and Maurice J. Elias) The Haworth Press, Inc., 1993, pp. 159-177. Multiple copies of this article/chapter may be purchased from The Haworth Document Delivery Center [1-800-3-HAWORTH; 9:00 a.m. - 5:00 p.m. (EST)].

phasis on a special education setting serving an urban, multi-ethnic population. Caveats based on experiences with institutionalizing a social and affective problem-solving group intervention are provided, as are some solutions.

Within the past decade, the affective and social development of students has become increasingly important to school based professionals. Social and affective functioning has been related to school adjustment and academic success (Forman, 1987) as well as to positive interpersonal relationships (Elias & Allen, 1992). The school environment which provides a context for children's academic learning and social/interpersonal interactions emerges as a logical and appropriate arena in which to address the social and affective functioning of students (Forman, 1987).

Within this context, school-based professionals are faced with a large number of students who could benefit from services and a small number of "helpers." Usually there are only 1 or 2 professional helpers per school, consisting of any combination of school psychologist, social worker, or guidance counselor, while the number of students ranges anywhere from 100-2000. Therefore, it seems reasonable that the most effective way to reach the most students would be to implement programs which target groups of students rather than individuals (Albee, 1982). Maher and Zins (1987a) describe three methods by which interventions may occur in a school setting. These include: a "one to one mode" (p. 3) consisting of direct service between a practitioner and a student; a "group mode which refers to direct service to two or more students by a practitioner" (p. 3), and a "consultation mode," which refers to indirect services to more than one student by a practitioner acting as a consultant to either teachers or parents. This consultative mode is supported by Albee (1982) and other community psychologists as an effective means of providing services to a larger number of people than can be served by either the one-to-one or group mode.

Much literature exists describing specific social and affective interventions which can be implemented within the schools. This body of literature (Carlson, 1987; Maher & Zins, 1987b; Reynolds & Stark, 1987; Urbain & Kendall, 1980; Zaragoza, Vaughn & McIntosh, 1991) primarily provides outlines of programs to be implemented and some outcome data. The outlines consist of session-by-session descriptions of the main topics covered and the main intervention modalities used. At times, the literature provides some specific directions for implementation, usually in the form of discovering problems faced in the course of running the program.

Rarely addressed, however, are processes of stabilization or institutionalization of an intervention. Ehly (this volume) expresses this point by listing *treatment integrity* as one of the four essential concerns that define the impact of an intervention. Treatment integrity must be viewed in a broad perspective by providers to special services in the schools, for providers will have a difficult time closely monitoring all of the interventions they put in place. Particularly when working in a consultative mode, providers need ways of ensuring that consultees will not only embrace interventions, but collaborate in a spirit of renewal to ensure interventions are sustained and modified as needed to reform, or augment, their effectiveness.

Commins and Elias (1991), in a review of the literature on organizational innovation, propose three stages through which an innovation or intervention progresses. The first is the *adoption phase,* where the organization/school learns about a particular intervention and decides to implement it. The second is the *implementation phase,* which consists of the intervention being put into use, and the third phase is when the intervention becomes stabilized within the organization or school. This phase, which encompasses a process to ensure treatment integrity, is referred to as the *institutionalization phase.*

Surprisingly, little attention has been given to the institutionalization phase of school based interventions. This phase is a complex phase which often seems simpler to achieve than it actually is. Often, the assumption is made that if implementation has occurred successfully, institutionalization will occur successfully, as well. This is not the case (Zins, 1992).

School based professionals are faced with the difficulty of institutionalization on a daily basis. Whether providing services in a one to one mode or group intervention mode, eventually the time arrives when the practitioner steps back from providing intervention services. This usually occurs due to the press of other duties and demands. De facto, the professional "hopes" and "assumes" the system will institutionalize the intervention. The system can be defined as the family unit, the classroom, all primary grades, the elementary school, the district or any other agency characterized by "rules, roles, relationships, activities and boundaries" (Fine, 1985; p. 263). Once an intervention has been introduced and begun successfully in a classroom, the question remains as to how to facilitate stabilization of that intervention so that its utilization remains likely despite the practitioner's absence, or at least a significant reduction in consultative attention.

This article focuses on the process of moving from the implementation phase to the institutionalization phase. Specifically, it addresses a common problem faced by special services providers/professional staff: how to move a group-based, teacher-led program from implementation to institutionalization. The perspective taken is that institutionalization must be planned for from the beginning of the program development and consultative process. Just as addressing pre-entry issues prior to the provision of consultative services is recommended, there are some specific structures and guidelines which may facilitate institutionalization of programs. This is important because considerations that might favor short-term implementation are not always those that favor institutionalization (Elias & Clabby, 1992). Therefore, a set of guidelines for successfully facilitating institutionalization is derived from the literature for use by those planning and/or consulting to group-based, teacher-led interventions. Specific illustrations are drawn from case examples of a multi-year social decision making and social problem solving intervention, with particular emphasis on procedures found to be effective for special education populations and settings.

Description of the social decision making and social problem solving program (SDMPS). The SDMPS program addresses the social and affective needs of students. It is a specific curriculum for elementary grades which is designed to foster the development of social/interpersonal decision making skills in children and adolescents. The curriculum uses a social-cognitive approach to teach social problem solving, including the areas of self control and social awareness, an eight step social decision making process, and the application of the above to content areas across the curriculum and routines and situations throughout the school day (Elias & Clabby, 1989). In a typical circumstance, a special services provider/professional staff member would attend a training in this approach and then return to the school to "turn-key" the program to the rest of the staff. The professional would organize and provide training, as well as follow-up consultation to ensure effective use of the program in the implementation phase. Thus, the model is what Maher and Zins (1989) would refer to as a consultative mode.

GUIDELINES AND STRUCTURES AIDING INSTITUTIONALIZATION OF GROUP INTERVENTIONS

Across a long history of group interventions in the schools, a common problem that must be confronted is that which focuses on the process of stabilization and institutionalization, or the preservation of treatment integrity. A related goal is to support an intervention within the school so that the program can be maintained without outside consultative services. This task, although always complex, is even more challenging in special education settings, especially to the extent to which children's problems are severe, the turnover rate of students and staff is high, and the flow of focal problems brought in by different cohorts of students changes. There can be a natural inclination to take steps to get an intervention going, including an urge to "do it oneself" as a way of minimizing administrative and bureaucratic hassles. However, a sufficient amount has been learned about institutionalization to make it clear that some early "short cuts" compromise long-term effectiveness and success. We present some of these learnings in the form of "guidelines" derived from the literature. Following this, we present a set of consultative *structures* that we have found valuable in helping to operationalize these guidelines and provide vehicles for special services providers/professional staff to use when working to institutionalize teacher-led group interventions such as SDMPS.

Guidelines for Achieving Institutionalization

Whether an intervention is established as a one to one mode (the professional and one student), a group mode (the professional and a group of students) or a consultative mode, there comes a time in the process when the professional moves out of the intervention, expecting the maintenance and development of the implementation process to continue within the system. For example, a school psychologist who introduces a peer tutoring intervention into a classroom expects that the intervention will stabilize while he/she is involved, and be maintained when she/he is no longer in the room on a daily basis. A consultant who works with a teacher to develop and implement a behavior management program in the classroom, works to insure that the behavior management program becomes routine and part of the teacher's repertoire in the classroom environment "so that it will continue to be successfully maintained by the teacher when the consultant is no longer available to provide ongoing support. In each of the above examples, the professional is performing in a way which increases the likelihood that the intervention will be institutionalized. What is the professional doing?

We examined the literature to find procedures supported in research or practice concerning their effectiveness in moving from the implementation of any group-oriented, school-based intervention to the establishment of that intervention in the system within which it exists. From these procedures, we have been able to derive a set of eight, encompassing guidelines to be used from the earliest stages of program planning and development to maximize the degree of institutionalization of programs.

(1) The goals of the intervention are consistent with the personal and professional values of the implementers (Commins & Elias, 1991; Hord, Rutherford, Huling-Austin, 1987; Huberman & Miles, 1984; Maher & Bennett, 1984; Sarason, 1982). Interventions are successful when those implementing it see its value and worth. Schools employ many interventions which are frequently competing with each other. An intervention perceived as consistent with the implementer's values is most likely to be accepted. Teachers are likely to invest time utilizing interventions which they believe will help develop their students' skills as well as develop their teaching abilities.

(2) Persons expected to carry out interventions must know what is expected of them (Brophy, 1988; Maher & Bennett, 1984; Zins & Ponti, 1990). Expectations must be clearly delineated and described.

Implementers should understand program requirements in terms of time, documentation, communication, and meetings. For long-term success, programmatic expectations are clearly and frequently articulated throughout the implementation process, and remain relatively consistent; radical changes often suggest a re-entry into the implementation phase, and should be treated as such. In particular, implementers should be given adequate time to discuss their role definitions. Once these role definitions are clear, they should be formally documented and disseminated so that particular and common roles are understood by those involved. Such documentation is best presented as an evolving document, with periodic revisions occurring based on formative evaluation, especially before the start of each academic year.

(3) The program/intervention must be securely in place (Hord et al., 1987; Huberman & Miles, 1984). The success or failure of a school based program often depends on the receptivity of the school staff to the program. Implementers must see value in its applicability. They must develop a desire to utilize component parts of the program and implement the intervention as it was intended to be implemented. This occurs when the program is well endorsed by both administration and staff; when adequate consultative support is provided to the implementers throughout the implementation phase, and when the implementers are able to develop a sense of mastery, confidence and control over program implementation.

(4) Administrative support must be established and maintained (Commins & Elias, 1991; Huberman & Miles, 1984; Maher & Bennett, 1984; Sarason, 1982). Administrative support must be available at all levels. This includes building support, district support, and board of education support. Institutionalized interventions become incorporated into local regulations or local procedures. Conducting group-based interventions in the classroom becomes part of the teachers' or special services providers' job descriptions. When an intervention is classroom based, the teacher presents it as part of weekly curricula or classroom rules. If an intervention is implemented on a school wide basis, the principal endorses it and documents it as a school policy. Additionally, one can see visible signs of consistent administrative pressure to implement the program. School personnel are encouraged to believe that the program

is a priority to the principal and considered consistent with the school's implicit or stated mission. Because principals consider the program valuable, they will relieve other requirements so that personnel can receive the training and coaching needed to successfully and enthusiastically implement the program. It must not be seen as "something extra to do which will help the students." In addition, there needs to exist a relative degree of administrator-teacher harmony.

(5) A core group of program implementers must be established (Elias & Clabby, 1984; Sarason, 1972; 1982). A core group consists of professionals in the system who are defined as leaders with regard to a particular program. The main function of the core group is to exist as the governing body, responsible for programmatic innovations, changes, and decisions. A core group can be established in a variety of ways. Sometimes it is based on members of the system who have prior experience or training with the specific program (i.e., a pilot group of teachers). A core group can be defined by administrators, or it can be peer nominated. The core group should demonstrate enthusiasm and support for the use of the program; be viewed by their peers as qualified and competent; demonstrate leadership qualities; and be willing to act as a decision making group for any issues related to implementation, stabilization or institutionalization, or expansion of the program.

(6) Appropriate opportunities for communication among implementers must be provided (Commins & Elias, 1991; Maher 1984; Sarason, 1982; Zins, 1992). Support for use of the program is communicated by peers as well as administration. Opportunities are available for implementers to discuss successes, failures, challenges possible adaptations and other concerns. Members outside of the core group are encouraged to believe their input is valuable, useful and seriously considered. They are provided with opportunities to collaborate with the core group either informally or formally. Administrators also are available to hear the successes and concerns of school personnel and are empathic, genuine, and responsive when addressing the staff's concerns.

(7) All attempts to refine, integrate, and adapt materials should be supported (Elias & Clabby, 1992; Huberman & Miles, 1984; Maher, 1984; Zins, 1992). The implementers must have a sense of ownership for the program. This often occurs by implementers developing or

utilizing new but related materials in the context of the program. Any attempts to adapt the program to more adequately meet the implementers' needs, while still fitting with the basic tenets of the program are supported and encouraged. Each system, be it a classroom, school, or individual, tends to need specific adaptations for a given program to be effective. Developing a system-specific operating manual or implementation guide which incorporates implementer-made materials, adaptations, and suggestions works to facilitate ownership of the program, create enthusiasm, and stimulate creativity in its implementers. This is of particular importance when tailoring a program to particular ethnic backgrounds, learning styles, or socio-emotional levels of children.

(8) Active work is taken to lower any resistances (Elias & Clabby, 1984; Huberman & Miles, 1984; Sarason, 1982). With the introduction of any new program, resistance of some kind can be expected. Any serious resistance which can work to sabotage institutionalization must be identified and targeted for change. Members of the core group are enthusiastic and accepting of the program and tend to be the source of input against resistances and its goals. The position of the core group as "insiders" willing to provide a reasonable amount of assistance to implementers enhances credibility. Implementers generally are open to accepting assistance which is readily and continuously available and offered.

Summary. The guidelines presented do not exist in a hierarchical fashion. Similarly, they are not employed in a linear fashion but are viewed as iterative and reflexive and are continuously addressed during the process of institutionalization. Rarely does reported research or practice address all of the elements contained in the guidelines. Nevertheless, they serve as a starting point for those concerned with setting up a group intervention that is likely to be sustained with integrity while their primary attentions are elsewhere. The use of these guidelines individually, and in combination, has guided actions taken in multiple settings to implement the SDMPS program in ways that have endured over many years (Elias & Clabby, 1992).

Structural "Solutions" to Intervention Problems

During our work, we have found that the presence of certain procedures has made it more likely that institutionalization will occur. These procedures can be thought of as structures that someone developing, managing, or consulting to a teacher-led classroom-based group intervention would want to put in place. There has been one setting in which a variety of structures have been put into place early in the program development process. It is a private school in New Jersey primarily for children classified emotionally disturbed with secondary learning impairments of various degrees of severity. The school serves approximately 125 students ages 4-13 from over ten different school districts; 69% of the students are from urban areas and ethnicities of students include 50% White, 39% Black, 8% Hispanic, and 3% Asian. Ten percent of the students are girls. In addition to teachers and teacher assistants in every classroom, one social worker is assigned for every three classes and every child receives individual therapy. Additionally, there are three crisis workers in the school that are employed to support teachers when the teachers believe a child is too distracting or disruptive to the children to remain in the classroom. These crisis workers are described as "problem solvers." Finally, the school also employs a music teacher, art teacher, gym teacher, computer teacher, speech teachers, a nurse and a librarian. The school has embarked on a 5 year pilot project with the intention of implementing the social decision making curriculum school-wide. To date, an SDMPS curriculum has been implemented in 12 classrooms in the school.

Program development and implementation. During the first year of implementation, six teachers and their assistants, the social workers, crisis workers, speech teachers, and specialists were trained in the implementation of the program. A specific school based curriculum, consisting of lessons which had been revised and adapted to adequately meet the needs of the students in this school, was created by teachers for school wide dissemination.

Consultation was provided one day per week by a school psychologist working with the Social Problem Solving Unit of the University of Medicine and Dentistry of New Jersey-Community Mental Health Center at Piscataway (UMDNJ-SPS) and Rutgers University. Weekly consultation services were provided to school personnel and administration including arranging on-site trainings by SPS Unit consultants and the on site consultant and advanced trainings conducted by UMDNJ-SPS and Rutgers University for experienced practitioners involved in the use of the curriculum across multiple sites in New Jersey and elsewhere throughout the United States.

Upon completion of the first year of implementation, six teachers had utilized the social decision making curriculum to address the self control, social awareness and social problem solving needs of their students. Most of the teachers were connected to the program; assumed a sense of ownership for it; were interested in adapting and modifying aspects of the curriculum to more effectively meet the needs of their students; and expressed positive reactions towards the intervention's usefulness. Consultative services were frequently available and utilized.

Plans for the second year of implementation included doubling the number of teachers involved in curriculum use, while simultaneously decreasing consultation time. The pressures of expansion, reducing consultation, and working in a special education environment make this setting an excellent example of how the guidelines were used to put into place the following structures, toward the goal of stabilizing the group intervention. We will draw on the Stabilizing Interventions example of this setting frequently, while sharing more general considerations across SDMPS sites (Elias & Clabby, 1992).

Mentor-mentee groupings. Mentor-mentee groupings are created in response to two primary problems. First, with expansion of an intervention to a school-wide level there are an increased number of school personnel implementing the SDMPS program which increases the amount of consultative time required. Second, expansion creates the condition of numerous personnel with varying levels of exposure/experience in the use of the SDMPS program. These different levels of expertise needed to be adequately addressed. Mentor-mentee groupings provide a viable means for insuring ongoing, informal feedback and consultation services.

Mentor-mentee groupings couple previously trained teachers (mentors) with a group of new implementers (mentees). The groupings are created based on class similarity in term of age, language ability, and cognitive ability. Typically, a "grouping" consists of two mentors and a small group of mentees. Contacts between groupings can occur at scheduled times, or informally. In the special educational setting described above, informal contacts between mentor-mentee groupings occurred frequently during teachers' preparatory periods, lunch, conversations in the hallways and morning commutes. More formal meeting times were created and scheduled during regular staff meeting time.

Implementer meetings. Teachers need a formal time to share ideas, provide and receive feedback, and support each others' implementation efforts. Implementer meetings provide this time while facilitating communication within implementers in the school community. Implementer meetings are typically co-led by mentors and consultants. In one special education setting, implementer meetings were scheduled every six weeks during part of the regular staff meetings. During this time, the school divided into smaller groups (i.e., primary and secondary). These meetings were led by mentors and consultants collaboratively and consisted of implementers sharing ideas and problems and helping each other brainstorm potential solutions to these problems.

Multidisciplinary team. An additional problem in the process of institutionalization is fostering independent implementation and maintenance of the SDMPS program by school personnel. Our solution to this problem is the creation of multidisciplinary team (MDT). MDT's consist of one member from each discipline within the school. For example, in our special education setting the MDT consisted of one teacher and one assistant from both the primary and secondary grades; one social worker, one crisis worker, one speech pathologist, and one specialist (i.e., art, music, or gym teacher). MDT members typically are volunteers and their participation on the team usually is sanctioned by school administrators. The team has a chairperson and is defined as the governing board for the SDMPS program. Representatives act as liaisons between their respective disciplines and the team. Meetings occur monthly and most often the content of these meetings refers to the progress and difficulties with curriculum used, specifically related to the areas of: (1) curriculum development (lessons developed and adapted material acquisition, flow of curriculum, use of videotapes); (2) structure of lessons, classroom management issues, scheduling and timing of lessons and social problem solving meetings; (3) integration of social problem solving into other areas (i.e., music, art, gym, computer, library, crisis workers, social workers); (4) coordination of mentoring; and (5) program expansion. In the special education setting described in this article, the MDT initially consisted of volunteers who were peer nominated. Although this "fit" with the school culture, this team had difficulty adopting a clearly defined role or making progress towards leadership. This was addressed by "re-electing" members of the team to more adequately reflect the core group, and switching the chairperson roles to individuals with direct administrative authority (school principal and chief school administrator).

Problem solving approach to management decisions. Schools often do not develop a consistent procedure to follow when reaching a roadblock in program implementation. Therefore, when a roadblock is stumbled upon, much time is spent attempting different solutions to the problem without a clear definition of what the problem is, or a clear understanding of a common goal. To address this issue, we use a problem solving approach to managerial decisions. The problem solving approach is consistent with the problem solving steps in the SDMPS program and consists of: clarifying feelings about the situation, defining the problem, defining the goal, brainstorming possible solutions and consequences, picking the best solution, making a final plan and trying it out, and evaluating progress and making modifications in the solution when necessary. Members of the school staff are actively taught these steps which are used throughout the school day. For example, in the special education setting the entire school staff was introduced to these steps at a staff meeting where the consultant and principal explained the process to the staff using everyday problems as examples. Additionally, the use of these steps for management decisions was reinforced and modeled by the MDT during their meetings.

Advanced training. Advanced trainings are conducted to address the problem arising from bringing new people into the implementation process of an already existing program. The trainings must respect the gains and skills of experienced implementers while simultaneously exposing new trainees to the component parts of the curriculum and over-arching skills necessary to implement the curriculum. For SDMPS, these skills include learning specific prompts the program uses to introduce self-control and social awareness skills, the process of teaching a skill, the specific problem solving steps the curriculum introduces, and the use of facilitative questioning which is a questioning technique used to help students think independently (Elias & Clabby, 1992). Training for experienced implementers focuses on the application of the problem solving steps to the content area as well as the elements necessary to be effective mentors and effective consultants. This includes, but is not limited to, defining the roles and responsibilities of mentors, facilitating communication between mentors and mentees, establishing collaborative relationships, and providing relevant reinforcement activities or additional resources. Additionally, some part of the training day is spent learning innovative intervention techniques developed in other, similar settings, and in applied practice. In our special education example, mentors and mentees were asked to work on adapting one lesson from the self-control or social awareness part of the curriculum, for their particular populations of students. Mentors additionally guided the mentees through the various curriculum materials collected by implementers in this and other special education settings.

Administrative renewal meetings. The problem of facilitating communication between administration, consultants, and school staff is addressed by administrative renewal meetings. These meetings occur approximately every three months and focus on re-establishing administrative support for the established structures and reasserting a commitment towards the direction of institutionalization. Time is spent defining common institutionalization goals and future directions, and progress towards full implementation and institutionalization is assessed. Resistances within the school are addressed and modifications in implementation procedures are developed.

Program evaluation. An ever-present problem in the implementation process is the absence of data to help administrative bodies (i.e., MDT's, administrative renewal meetings) make informed decisions regarding directions for ongoing program improvement. In response to this, program evaluation is conducted as an integral and ongoing part of the intervention process. To be most useful, program evaluation must focus not only on the outcomes of the program implemented, but also on the process of implementation (Maher, 1984). In the special education case example, two types of program evaluations are conducted. The first, is a mid-year evaluation of all structures and implementation procedures, to help address future adaptations necessary for success of the SDMPS program. The second evaluation, conducted at the end of the academic year, focuses on obtaining process data similar to the mid-year data but also on evaluating educational attainment (of implementers), directions of future training seminars, and outcome data related to program effectiveness. Prior baseline data or control group data are used where possible for comparison purposes. This information is used during the summer months to provide direction for fall implementation.

REFLECTIONS AND FUTURE DIRECTIONS

The guidelines have been used across a number of sites to help create the structures described. Additionally, they facilitate and shape the consultation process used to support the implementation and stabilization of teacher-led classroom-based group interventions. There are a general set of results found across sites (Elias & Clabby, 1992) which suggest that to the extent to which the structures are in place, longer-term implementation and progress towards stable, ongoing utilization of interventions follow.

In the special education school described earlier, by the end of the second year, 4 of the 8 guidelines had been built in strongly and the remaining four were in place and being implemented. Commins and Elias (1991) suggest that this early profile is a pathway toward successful institutionalization. In our example, the teacher-led classroom-based group intervention was being supported by a core group of program implementers (MDT) who had begun to take ownership for various program components such as curriculum development, the development of advanced trainings to occur in year 3, and lesson adaptation and modification. Administrative support increased tremendously, as evidenced by administration providing incentives for summer MDT meetings. Appropriate communication opportunities among implementers and administration were continuously provided and expectations for implementation were being clearly delineated during the summer MDT meetings for dissemination and discussion at the beginning of year 3.

Caveats for Service Providers

Although strong progress toward institutionalization may occur in the context of program implementation, it is important to recognize that it is a continuously evolving process. In spite of applying each guideline throughout the consultative process, one is likely to encounter barriers to institutionalization. What has greatly assisted us in our work is having the guidelines to use as consultative tools. Over the course of implementing group interventions in many school sites, typical problems on the rocky road toward institutionalization have been identified. We present some examples, drawn particularly from our experience in the previously described special education setting, to better ease the path for other consultants.

First, the impact of expansion must be carefully considered. Expansion from a few selected implementers to a significantly larger number of implementers will weaken the stability of the program. In our example, we misjudged the degree to which the addition of 6 classrooms would impact on the stability of the program. The program was securely in place at the start of the school year. The structures were initiated to explicate the administrative process in an effort to maintain the stability of the intervention. However, as additional teachers were trained in the program, these structures were not sufficient. Classrooms which had participated in the program remained stable in their use and implementation, but few developed further because the majority of the consultation focus was targeted towards stabilizing the new classrooms; progress toward institutionalization actually was impeded.

Second, consultants must be careful not to overestimate people's preparation for leadership roles, regardless of their enthusiasm and/or appropriateness for these roles. Core groups which develop naturally as a result of exposure/experience should be supported and their enthusiasm reinforced. The special education example described here supports this caveat. For example, in an attempt to work within the school culture, we had peers "nominate" a multidisciplinary team who would act as the core group. This nomination process resulted in a mixture of people, some of whom demonstrated high enthusiasm to the program, took initiative and assumed a decision making role, and others who demonstrated high resistance to the program and were not invested in further developing the SDMPS program. Using the mentors as the core group from the beginning would have eased these issues. The mentors already had feelings of ownership, were positive about the program, felt confident in their decision making abilities about the program, and informally adopted a leadership role. Ultimately, the multidisciplinary team was restructured to take this into consideration.

Third, addressing implementer expectations regarding the implementation process and providing opportunities for communication among implementers and between implementers, consultants and administration are imperative. Communication is a crucial aspect of successful program implementation. It cannot be assumed that implementers or administrators are aware of their roles and responsibilities are in program implementation and maintenance or that they are well informed as to the status of the program. Administrative renewal meetings create a structure for addressing this issue before it becomes a problem. In our special education setting, there were few administrative renewal meetings initially and administrative investment appeared to be wavering in light of the press of other demands.

For example, there were some structures that were in place which insured success according to our guidelines (such as teacher sharing meetings which were developed as avenues for teachers to provide each other with mutual support and encouragement while providing ideas for successful lesson adaptations) which were frequently canceled as a result of other systemic demands. Therefore, formal administrative renewal meetings were held to articulate mutual needs, define roles, and explicate expectations. During this time, important clarification of who was serving as the on-site program coordinator took place. Thus, administrative support was firmly established and the process began to flow more smoothly. These circumstances serve to remind consultants of Sarason's (1982) point that stabilization of school-based programs typically takes a minimum of three years, despite how quickly progress *seems* to occur.

CONCLUSION

The guidelines presented are just that–guidelines. Adherence to them does not ensure successful institutionalization; it does, however, appear to increase the likelihood that institutionalization will occur. Successfully establishing the structures described also does not insure successful institutionalization, but rather, significantly increases the likelihood that the guidelines will be achieved (which consequently facilitate institutionalization). Within any system, there is always a specific context which needs to be taken into account. This context may influence the way in which the practitioner embarks on implementation, stabilization, and institutionalization activities. We have used examples drawn from the implementation of a teacher-led group SDMPS intervention to illustrate ways in which the context and structures interact. By considering both the proposed guidelines and careful attention to systemic variables, special services providers/professional staff working with group interventions in schools can take on a more consultative role, increase the likelihood of continued programmatic implementation without direct consultative services, and therefore increase both the numbers of students receiving interventions and the level of their effectiveness.

REFERENCES

Albee, G. (1982). Preventing psychopathology and promoting human potential. *American Psychologist,* 1043-1050.

Brophy, J. (1986). Teacher influences on student achievement. *American Psychologist, 41,* 1069-1077.

Carlson, C.I. (1987). Helping students deal with divorce related issues. *Special Services in the Schools. 3,3/4,* 121-135.

Commins, W.W., Elias, M.J. (1991). Institutionalization of mental health programs in organizational contexts: The case of elementary schools. *Journal of Community Psychology, 19,* 207-220.

Elias, M.J., Allen, G.J. (1992). A comparison of instructional methods for delivering a preventive social competence/social decision making program to at risk, average, and competent students. *School Psychology Quarterly, 6,* 257-272.

Elias, M.J., Clabby, J.F. (1984). Integrating social and affective education into public school curriculum and instruction. In C.A. Maher, R.J. Illback, & J.E. Zins (Eds.), *Organizational psychology in the schools: A handbook for professionals* (pp. 143-172). Springfield, IL: C.C. Thomas.

Elias, M.J., Clabby, J.F. (1989). *Social decision-making skills.* Rockville, MD: Aspen.

Elias, M.J., Clabby, J.F. (1992). *Building social problem solving skills: Guidelines from a school-based program.* San Francisco: Jossey Bass.

Forman, S.G. (1987). Affective and social interventions in the schools. *Special Services in the Schools, 3, 3/4,* 1-5.

Hord, S., Rutherford, W., Huling-Austin, L., & Hall, G. (1987). *Taking charge of change.* Alexandria, VA: Association for Supervision and Curriculum Development.

Huberman, A.M., & Miles, M.B. (1984). *Innovation up close: How school improvement works.* New York: Plenum.

Maher, C.A. (1984). Description and evaluation of an approach to implementing program in organizational settings. *Journal of Organizational Behavior Management, 2,* 69-98.

Maher, C.A., & Bennett, R.E. (1984). *Planning and evaluating special education services.* Englewood Cliffs: Prentice Hall.

Maher, C.A., & Zins, J.E. (1987a). Framework for school based psychoeducational interventions. In C.A. Maher & J. E. Zins (Eds). *Psychoeducational interventions in the schools* (pp. 1-7). New York: Pergamon.

Maher, C.A., & Zins, J.E. (Eds). (1987b). *Psychoeducational interventions in the schools.* New York: Pergamon.

Reynolds, W.M., & Stark, K.D. (1987). School-based intervention strategies for the treatment of depression in children and adolescents. *Special Services in the Schools, 3, (3/4),* 69-88.

Sarason, S.B. (1972). *The creation of settings and the future societies.* San Francisco: Jossey Bass.

Sarason, S.B. (1982). *The culture of the school and the problem of change* (2nd Ed.). Boston: Allyn and Bacon.

Urbain, E.S., & Kendall, P.C. (1980). Review of social-cognitive problem-solving interventions with children. *Psychological Bulletin, 88,* 109-143.

Zaragoza, N., Vaughn, S., & McIntosh, R. (1991). Social skills interventions and children with behavior problems: A review. *Behavioral Disorders, 19,* 260-275.

Zins, J.E. (1992). Implementing school-based consultation services: An analysis of five years of practice. In R. Conyne & J. O'Neil (Eds.), *Casebook of Organizational Consultation. A casebook.* (pp. 50-79). Newbury Park, CA: Sage.

Zins, J.E., & Ponti, C.R. (1990). Best practices in school-based consultation. In A. Thomas & J. Grimes (Eds.), *Best practices in school psychology-II* (pp. 673-694). Washington, D.C.: National Association of School Psychologists.

Multicultural Issues in the Delivery of Group Interventions

Mary Jane Rotheram-Borus

University of California, Los Angeles

SUMMARY. Innovative preventive interventions are increasingly delivered in small group settings to children in school who are at risk for a variety of negative outcomes. In addition to reducing children's risk, these interventions present the possibility of enhancing students' awareness and understanding of cross-ethnic peers. To be effective with children from diverse ethnic backgrounds, these programs must examine their underlying assumptions regarding the definitions of social competence and methods of behavior change, tailor the program for each ethnic group served, and examine the impact of the interventions across different domains of the children's life.

Substantial progress has been made in demonstrating the effectiveness of preventive interventions in small group settings in

---

Address correspondence to: Dr. Mary Jane Rotheram-Borus, Department of Psychiatry, University of California, Los Angeles, 760 Westwood Plaza, Los Angeles, CA 90024-1759.

This paper was prepared with support from the W.T. Grant Foundation, Faculty Scholars Award, and a grant from the National Institute of Mental Health Grant No. HD2084001 and ME30903-07.

[Haworth co-indexing entry note]: "Multicultural Issues in the Delivery of Group Interventions." Rotheram-Borus, Mary Jane. Co-published simultaneously in *Special Services in the Schools*, (The Haworth Press, Inc.) Vol. 8, No. 1, 1993, pp. 179-188; and: *Promoting Student Success Through Group Interventions* (ed: Joseph E. Zins, and Maurice J. Elias) The Haworth Press, Inc., 1993, pp. 179-188. Multiple copies of this article/chapter may be purchased from The Haworth Document Delivery Center [1-800-3-HAWORTH; 9:00 a.m. - 5:00 p.m. (EST)].

schools, as evidenced by the interventions described in this volume. In schools, these programs are being delivered increasingly to children and adolescents from many ethnic groups in multicultural settings. Hispanic, African-American, Native-American, Chinese-American, Japanese-American, Eastern-European, and Vietnamese children are often found in the same classroom. Because there are substantial ethnic differences in the social behaviors, expectations, roles, values, and scripts of each ethnic groups, preventive interventions must be tailored to be consistent with the norms and background of the students who are participating. The goal of this paper is to review how students' ethnicity shapes the goals of preventive interventions, the methods of program implementation, and the impact of the programs.

PROGRAM EMPHASIS AND COMPATIBILITY WITH SOCIAL NORMS OF DIFFERENT ETHNIC GROUPS

There are substantial differences in the basic assumptions of the programs presented in this issue. The differences exist along several dimensions. One dimension is the degree to which these programs encourage development of children's cognitive, affective, or behavioral skills. For example, interpersonal problem solving is the backbone of Braswell's intervention program for children with disruptive behavior disorders. Thus, children's cognitive style of processing or failing to process social cues, generate alternatives, and evaluate the means-ends-consequences of the alternatives to solve problems changes when experiencing cognitive-behavioral intervention program of Braswell. These children are likely to become more active in their interpersonal encounters and take a proactive stance towards shaping their individual environment. In contrast, programs focused on recovery from a specific stressor, such as divorce and loss, presume that disclosure and discussions of feelings improve the quality of children's lives. There are even differences between divorce and loss programs: the intervention for children of divorce includes behavioral strategies for coping with specific issues that arise during the course of family dissolution; the bereavement program more narrowly focuses on the expression of feelings associated with anticipated events, such as funerals. In both programs, however, it is likely that children participating in these programs may increase their emotional expressiveness with others, including expressions of sadness and displeasure. Peer leadership training also involves the changes in how feelings are expressed and managed. In particular, adolescents are taught that group interactions will progress along a stage model. "Storming" or methods of conflict resolution are assumed to be part of every group process. Finally, Gresham and Elliott's intervention designed for enhancing social skills training teaches children to acquire verbal and nonverbal behaviors that are socially normative and likely to lead to social rewards.

The programs differentially emphasize thinking, feeling, or acting. However, each program is similar in providing children and adolescents with a map and set of social expectations directing them about how to understand their world. Yet, there are key questions: whose map is used to define this world? Which ethnic norms direct the design of the program? Social expectations that are taught may be consistent with or different from those provided by the children's parents, family, and community. Each prevention program adopts a view that individual children can actively think to shape their world, change their behavior, or increase awareness of their feelings in a manner consistent with that program's view of prevailing social norms. This stands in contrast to the "wait and see" or "turn to a higher force" philosophy which characterizes some cultures (Stewart, 1972). For example, some cultures expect problems to unfold around people without their personal action (Diaz-Guerrero, 1987). Other cultures endorse norms for strong individuality and high activity (see Rotheram & Phinney, 1987a, for a review; Rotheram-Borus & Tsemberis, 1989). Interpersonal problem solving training endorses these high activity norms, as do the norms for Black and White American children and adolescents (Kochman, 1981; Sagar & Schofield, 1980). Black and White children may, therefore, find programs that teach interpersonal problem solving skills compatible with their pre-existing styles. In contrast, Mexican- and Japanese-Americans often endorse norms that encourage a group orientation and a less active coping style (Knight & Kagan, 1982; Knudson, 1979). Mexican- and Japanese-American children may be less responsive to interventions programs that attempt to enhance interpersonal problem solving. An active, individualistic problem-solving approach can be inconsistent with the styles children have learned at home to solve problems and approach conflict. Difficulties in implementing interpersonal problem solving programs could also be anticipated for Hawaiian-American children who utilize family members and focus on immediate solutions when attempting to resolve problems (Gallimore, Boggs, & Jordan, 1974).

Ethnic differences in styles of emotional expressiveness present similar problems to children involved in small group interventions that attempt to facilitate resolution of emotional conflicts and distress. For example, Native-American children are not encouraged to express emotions publicly, particularly grief and distress with peers (Ainworth, 1984; Echohawk, 1978). Death, in particular, has very different meanings cross-culturally (Wyche & Rotheram-Borus, 1990). These meanings influence the emotional processing of these experiences and would likely influence children's response to bereavement and divorce intervention programs.

Finally, when placed in intervention groups that encourage behavioral skills, it is critical to identify whose behavioral norms are to be taught. Will children be taught to establish eye contact when scolded or to look to the floor? Ethnic groups differ widely on this behavior. Should assertiveness be taught? Such behaviors might be quite successful with middle-class White teachers in suburban neighborhoods; however, are they likely to be successful in inner-city settings or Hispanic barrios? There are no clear answers to these questions. However, ethnic differences in children's socialization around these actions will influence their responsiveness to intervention programs.

TAILORING INTERVENTIONS TO THE GROUP SERVED AND ENHANCING CROSS-ETHNIC UNDERSTANDING

Prevention programs are expected to be differentially successful based on ethnicity. Documented ethnic differences in attitudinal, affective, and behavioral patterns both across cultures (Whiting & Whiting, 1975) and within cultures (Forges, 1979) are not random, but are organized and dependent on the gestalt of a particular culture (Mo, 1982). To understand these differences, researchers have specified dimensions along which ethnic groups differ: (1) an active versus a passive manner of coping; (2) an orientation towards the group's goals (cooperative) versus an emphasis on the individual's goals and behaviors (competitive); (3) a norm of expressing one's emotions versus one of emotional restraint; and (4) deference to authority with relationships ordered in a hierarchical fashion versus a more egalitarian distribution of power (see Rotheram & Phinney, 1987a, for a review). What impact do these ethnic differences have on the implementation and success of small group intervention programs?

The impact of these programs has often been evaluated among middle class children, a factor that is confounded with ethnicity. Evaluation of the effectiveness of each program has not typically been conducted with non-mainstream children. When such evaluations are initiated, we must ask how exposure and encouragement to adopt specific coping strategies will impact the child's self perceptions. What is the impact of these programs on a child's ethnic identity and adjustment if children are taught mainstream norms for socially competent behavior? Will the child be bicultural? What impact does biculturalism have on adjustment?

It has been documented that children are labeled and are aware of their ethnicity by about age 5-8 (see Rotheram & Phinney, 1987b, for a review). Simultaneously cross-ethnic attitudes are being established during this developmental period. By early adolescence children have chosen a reference group, i. e., a group to serve as their standard for self-valuation. In multicultural settings, children are clearly exposed to the norms, values, and expectations of cross-ethnic peers. However, if the children participate in intervention programs that endorse mainstream norms and values, how will this impact the child's identity development?

There has been much controversy regarding these questions, but little empirical evidence to guide program decisions. The controversy has centered primarily on the impact of biculturalism in children. Biculturalism refers to the ability to negotiate two cultures simultaneously, with an awareness of the norms of both cultures. There have been no assessments of the relationship of biculturalism and preventive intervention programs. Rotheram and Phinney (1987a), however, have found ethnic differences in the social expectations of Black and Mexican-American children in the same, integrated classroom. Children whose expectations were highly similar to their group reported higher self-esteem, indicating the importance of maintaining the patterns of one's ethnic group. However, identification solely with one's ethnic group is also likely to have costs. Hispanic children must learn English in order to succeed in the economic marketplace of the United States. In addition to speaking English, Hispanic children must be aware of mainstream norms and able to negotiate mainstream culture. If they do not learn these norms, children will be at a disadvantage in the work place later.

Do ethnic differences affect some types of training programs more than others? If one is focusing on training behavioral skills, the potential for conflict in behavioral repertoires is clear. If Hispanic children are taught to look adults in the eyes when in trouble, the children are learning patterns that are likely to elicit punishment in their own community. Reflecting sensitivity ethnicity, Gresham and Elliott's program, the most behavioral intervention presented in this issue, focuses on the behavioral principles that are associated with behavior change. Rather than teaching specific behaviors, methods of enhancing behavior change are detailed (e.g., modeling, rehearsal). Programs that teach interpersonal problem solving, such as Braswell's program for hyperactivity, also claim that specific content is not taught, but the process of thinking about problems is stressed (Spivack & Shure, 1976). However, the belief that one actively identifies and seeks to act on interpersonal problems reflects an active mode of responding. This is one of the basic dimensions along which ethnic groups differ. There is no single answer to the question of how ethnicity differentially shapes or is shaped by intervention programs. It is a question which practitioners must always keep in mind, however.

The relevance of cultural considerations on group interventions must be extended so as to not underestimate their potential benefits to increase cross-ethnic understanding. All programs described by the various contributors allow and encourage children to discuss their interpersonal relationships and enhance skills to engage in such discussions. These groups offer an opportunity for children to identify ethnic differences in social expectations in a warm, supportive atmosphere. These school-based group interventions allow exploration of these differences and allow students to identify the gap that often exists between positive social intentions and misunderstood actions. For example, Black children and adolescents are likely to be perceived by their White peers as more aggressive in ambiguous situations (Sagar & Schofield, 1980). Aggressive feelings and actions are likely to precipitate a fair amount of conflict in multi-ethnic group interventions because the social expectations of Black and White children and adolescents are likely to be different. Meeting in small groups allows students to discover differences in their expectations in non-threatening settings. This is an important social benefit of these programs.

DIFFERENTIAL IMPACT OF PROGRAMS ACROSS DOMAINS: SCHOOL, HOME, NEIGHBORHOOD, CHURCH

Ethnic differences are likely to have differential impact in various domains of a student's life. For example, one of the best programs described in this volume addressed social skills training. "Being socially competent," the targeted outcome of this program, is a judgment usually based on the evaluation of more than one person, often measured by peers' and teachers' ratings of children (Asher, Singleton, & Taylor 1982). How does this evaluation vary when the cultural background of the evaluated person varies from that of the evaluator? When an Anglo teacher evaluates a Mexican-American child, whose norms are used to define social competence? The evaluation will be in the eyes of the beholder.

Few programs consider the impact of the four primary units of socialization–the family, schools, peers, and community agencies. Yet, it seems likely that certain group intervention programs may differentially impact adjustment in different areas of the child's life (Rotheram-Borus, in press). For example, Mexican-American children are taught to lower their eyes as a means of showing respect to elders. Anglo teachers are likely to expect that children will look directly into the eyes of an authority figure, especially when chastised. If we teach Mexican-American children to look others in the eyes, what is likely to happen when children engage in this behavior with their families? How will White and Mexican-American children interact on the playground if each has different social expectations of socially appropriate behavior? It can be valuable to keep these considerations in mind and address them during the course of the group interventions. The kinds of structures for stabilizing group interventions described by Robinson and Elias provide opportunities and vehicles for group leaders to raise these issues and share possible ways to minimize cross-domain conflicts or resolve those that do occur.

CONCLUSION

Small group interventions can create opportunities for children from many ethnic groups to increase their understanding of the norms, values, and social routines of their cross-ethnic peers. The small group setting offers the opportunity to become aware of ethnic differences in social expectations. A gap often exists between a child's social intentions and the impact of that child's behavior on his/her cross-ethnic peers. Rather than perpetuating misunderstanding, children become aware of their own assumptions regarding social relationships, as well as the expectations of their peers in small group settings. This is a potential advantage–often an unintentional advantage–of small group interventions in schools. In particular, minority children may have the opportunity to "code switch," i.e., to change their social repertoire depending on their social setting. When interacting with their families, children can adopt the norms of their families' ethnic group. When at school with cross-ethnic peers, children can demonstrate the behaviors needed to succeed socially with theme peers. Similar adjustments can be made in work places and other domains.

Simultaneously, those who are insensitive to cultural and ethnic norms in the design and implementation of small group interventions can create numerous conflicts for children. Children may acquire patterns that are different from their families' values and receive substantial negative feedback in non-school settings for these patterns. Children's expectations may narrow to endorse only one set of "positive" behaviors, even if these behaviors are incompatible with the norms of the child's ethnic group. This narrowness can lead children to feel bad about themselves when their actions or feelings vary from those endorsed at school. Children can be encourage to develop an "out-group" orientation, i. e., feeling more comfortable when dealing with others outside of their ethnic group.

Given the possibilities that exist, it is critical that school personnel consider the ethnic background of students participating in their programs and involve broad staff input and involvement of parents and community members in program development. Several authors in this volume advocate such an approach–Braswell, Kalter and Schreier, Powell, Robinson and Elias, and Ehly. By following the recommendations of the program developers, the full benefits of each of these intervention programs may be experienced by children of many ethnic groups.

REFERENCES

Ainworth, N. (1984). The cultural shaping of oral discourse. *Theory into Practice, 23*, 9, 132-137.

Asher, S.R., Singleton, L.C., & Taylor, A.R. (1982, March). *Acceptance versus friendship: A longitudinal study of racial integration.* Paper presented at the annual meeting of the American Educational Research Association, New York.

Diaz-Guerrero, R. (1987). Ethnic patterns among Mexican-American children. In J. Phinney & Rotheram, M.J. *Children's ethnic socialization: Pluralism and development.* Newbury Park, CA: Sage.

Echohawk, L. (1978). Locus of control among American Indian youth. *Dissertation Abstracts International, 38*, (9-B), 4450-4452.

Forges, J. (1979). *Social episodes.* New York: Academic Press. Gallimore, R., Boggs, J. & Jordan, C. (1974). *Culture, behavior, and education.* Beverly Hills, CA: Sage.

Knight, G., & Kagan, S. (1982). Siblings, birth order, and cooperative-competitive social behavior: A comparison of Anglo-American children of two ages. *Journal of Cross-Psychology, 13, 239-240.*

Knudson, K. (1979). The relationships among affective role-taking, empathy, and prosocial behavior in a sample of Mexican-American and Anglo-American children of two ages. *Dissertation Abstracts International 39* (8)b, 1042.

Kochman, T. (1981). *Black and white styles in conflict.* Chicago: University of Chicago Press.

Mo, J. (1982). Socialization: A cultural ecological approach. In K. Borman (Ed.), *The social life of children in a changing society.* Hillsdale, NJ: Erlbaum.

Rotheram, M. J., & Phinney, J. (1987a). Introduction: Definitions and processes. In J. Phinney & M.J. Rotheram (Eds.), *Children's ethnic socialization: Pluralism and development.* Newbury Park, CA: Sage.

Rotheram, M. J., & Phinney, J. (1987b). Ethnic behavior problems as an aspect of identity. In J. Phinney & M.J. Rotheram (Eds.), *Children's ethnic socialization: Pluralism and development.* Newbury Park, CA: Sage.

Rotheram-Borus, M. J. (in press). Biculturalism among adolescents: Impact and development. In M. Bernal & G. Knight (Eds.), *Formation and transmission of ethnic identity in children.* Tempe, AZ: University of Arizona Press.

Rotheram-Borus, M.J., & Tsemberis, S. (1989). The role of ethnicity in social competency training programs. In L. Bond & B. Compass (Eds.), *Primary prevention and promotion in the schools* (pp. 297-318). Newbury Park, CA: Sage.

Sagar, H. & Schofield, J. (1980). Racial and behavioral cues in Black and White children's perceptions of ambiguously aggressive acts. *Journal of Personality and Social Psychology, 39, 590-598.*

Spivack, G., & Shure, M.B., (1974). *Social adjustment of young children: A cognitive approach to solving real-life problems.* San Francisco: Jossey-Bass.

Stewart, E. (1972). *American cultural patterns: A cross-cultural perspective.* Chicago: Intercultural Press.

Whiting, B., & Whiting, J. (1975). *Children of six cultures: A psycho-cultural analysis.* Cambridge, MA: Harvard University Press.

Wyche, K., & Rotheram-Borus, M.J. (1990). Ethnic difference in adolescent suicidal behavior. In A. Stiffman (Ed.), *Advances in psychiatry* (Vol. 18, pp. 323-338). Beverly Hills, CA: Sage.

Haworth DOCUMENT DELIVERY SERVICE

and Local Photocopying Royalty Payment Form

This new service provides (a) a single-article order form for any article from a Haworth journal and (b) a convenient royalty payment form for local photocopying (not applicable to photocopies intended for resale).

- *Time Saving:* No running around from library to library to find a specific article.
- *Cost Effective:* All costs are kept down to a minimum.
- *Fast Delivery:* Choose from several options, including same-day FAX.
- *No Copyright Hassles:* You will be supplied by the original publisher.
- *Easy Payment:* Choose from several easy payment methods.

Open Accounts Welcome for . . .

- Library Interlibrary Loan Departments
- Library Network/Consortia Wishing to Provide Single-Article Services
- Indexing/Abstracting Services with Single Article Provision Services
- Document Provision Brokers and Freelance Information Service Providers

MAIL or *FAX* THIS ENTIRE ORDER FORM TO:

Attn: **Marianne Arnold**
Haworth Document Delivery Service
The Haworth Press, Inc.
10 Alice Street
Binghamton, NY 13904-1580

or FAX: (607) 722-1424
or CALL: 1-800-3-HAWORTH
(1-800-342-9678; 9am-5pm EST)

PLEASE SEND ME PHOTOCOPIES OF THE FOLLOWING SINGLE ARTICLES:

1) Journal Title: ______________________________
Vol/Issue/Year: ______________ Starting & Ending Pages: ______________
Article Title: ______________________________
____

2) Journal Title: ______________________________
Vol/Issue/Year: ______________ Starting & Ending Pages: ______________
Article Title: ______________________________
____

3) Journal Title: ______________________________
Vol/Issue/Year: ______________ Starting & Ending Pages: ______________
Article Title: ______________________________
____

4) Journal Title: ______________________________
Vol/Issue/Year: ______________ Starting & Ending Pages: ______________
Article Title: ______________________________
____

(See other side for Costs and Payment Information)

COSTS: Please figure your cost to order quality copies of an article.

1. Set-up charge per article: $8.00
   ($8.00 × number of separate articles) __________
2. Photocopying charge for each article:
   1-10 pages: $1.00 __________
   11-19 pages: $3.00 __________
   20-29 pages: $5.00 __________
   30+ pages: $2.00/10 pages __________
3. Flexicover (optional): $2.00/article __________
4. Postage & Handling: US: $1.00 for the first article/
   $.50 each additional article __________
   Federal Express: $25.00 __________
   Outside US: $2.00 for first article/
   $.50 each additional article __________
5. Same-day FAX service: $.35 per page __________
6. Local Photocopying Royalty Payment: should you wish to copy the article yourself. Not intended for photocopies made for resale. $1.50 per article per copy
   (i.e. 10 articles x $1.50 each = $15.00) __________

GRAND TOTAL: ____________

METHOD OF PAYMENT: (please check one)

❏ Check enclosed ❏ Please ship and bill. PO # ________________
(sorry we can ship and bill to bookstores only! All others must pre-pay)

❏ Charge to my credit card: ❏ Visa; ❏ MasterCard; ❏ American Express;

Account Number: ________________ Expiration date: ________

Signature: ✗ ________________ Name: ________________

Institution: ________________ Address: ________________

City: ________________ State: ________ Zip: ________

Phone Number: ________________ FAX Number: ________________

MAIL or *FAX* THIS ENTIRE ORDER FORM TO:

Attn: **Marianne Arnold**
Haworth Document Delivery Service
The Haworth Press, Inc.
10 Alice Street
Binghamton, NY 13904-1580

or FAX: (607) 722-1424
or CALL: 1-800-3-HAWORTH
(1-800-342-9678; 9am-5pm EST)